DOGGIE STYLE

The truth about what it takes to be the Top
Dog in any relationship!

DOGGIE STYLE

The truth about what it takes to be the Top
Dog in any relationship!

Steven Eric Scruggs

The personal stories listed in this book are true. Only the names have been changed to protect the innocent and the not-so innocent.

All cartoons by Steven Eric Scruggs

First Printing 2001

ISBN: 1-58820-368-9

This book is printed on acid free paper.

1stBooks – rev. 7/9/01

What Everybody's Saying About This Book!

" I can't believe anybody would have the nerve to say some of the stuff I'm reading in this book!"---- Carolyn, from New Orleans.

"This book is blowin' up! It's the Bomb! When is the movie coming out!?"---- Ralph, from Detroit.

"All I can say is you sure better read it before your man does!"--- Tamia, from Memphis.

"We women aren't really like that, Are we?"---- Lori, from Los Angeles.

"This book is going to make a whole lot of people angry! I'd advise anybody who's afraid of new and controversial ideas to not buy this book!"---- Warren, from Atlanta.

"This book has probably changed the way I look at dating forever. It's funny and deep, both at the same time!"----Rena, from Dallas.

Acknowledgements

I would like to give special thanks to all my friends and family for all the love, support, and patience they have so graciously shown me during the time it took me to write this book. I love you all dearly. Without you in my life, this would have been a lot more difficult to complete.

I would also, even more importantly, like to thank my Lord Jesus Christ for all the love, courage, and inspiration that He has given me throughout my writing this book. I love Him dearly because He first loved me. Without Him, there would be no me.

Table of Contents

Introduction

Men and women. Boys and girls. Whether you are standing on a bus or a subway train, sitting in a chair or lying on a couch or a bed and you are holding this book in your hands, you have obviously come to face with the reality that trying to understand the opposite sex dominates much of our lives. This may come as a surprise to many of us. This may even qualify to many of us as a major revelation. In writing this book, my research has uncovered that people usually fall into two categories as far as relationship skills are concerned. There are those who have either got it going on and don't know why, or those who've got it going to the dogs and they also don't know why. As you can see there is a fine line of contrast between the two. The one thing that is universally consistent is that many times neither of these two groups exactly know why they are either failing or succeeding at maintaining the quality of the love relationships that they hold so dearly. In, fact that's what this book is about. It was written to help you in opening your eyes by revealing to you tried and true techniques and strategies on how to attain and maintain happy, fulfilling romantic relationships.

Let's face it, we are living in a time where every fact of life is becoming more and more complicated. Computer technology is taking over. Everything is becoming more and more automated, less personal. Although we have the Internet, which can be used as a great tool to communicate with people all around the world, its still painfully evident that it is the one on one communication between the sexes that remains so difficult. Indeed, understanding between male and female to any real useful degree continues to be elusive in the frantic hurry up and wait culture in which we live. That men and women are different is a statement that should go without saying with the relentless bombardment of countless amounts of "helpful" books, tapes, and seminars being rained down upon us by many well-meaning psychologists and psychotherapists who are enjoying so much popularity these days. This clutter of pseudointellectual information should be easily recognizable to anyone who has perused their neighborhood book store desperately searching for anything that will help them either find the love of their lives, or save the life in their loves. You know them when you see them. They're the ones with the authors and titles that can be easily interchangeable, because they all talk about things like "Shaking your romantic co-independency", "Embracing your dysfunctional, inner love child", and last but not least, "Ten ways to save your relationship thru neurological, emotional programming made easy". What any of this has to do with getting what you want out of a relationship is anybody's guess. I'm here to say enough already. Enough with the pop-psychology. Enough with the endless psycho babble. What we really need is honest-to-goodness straight talk in colloquial terms that everybody can understand. What we all have been yearning for is a clear, concise message that shows you how to find the love you want, how to make your love life satisfying, and most importantly, how to make it last.

Inspiration for writing this book came to me suddenly one Saturday a few short years ago. It happened while attending a charity sponsored picnic populated by many of my friends and co-workers. On the surface it was about fun and games, and generally having a good time. Unbeknownst to everyone, although I too was smiling on the outside, on the inside I was still reeling in disbelief from the tragic ending of a romantic relationship I was involved in up until a few nights prior. My world felt like it had ended not with a bang, but with a whimper. On paper, and probably to the casual observer, me and my lady seemed very compatible and meant for each other. However, over the course of the time we spent together, it became increasingly clear that I loved her much more than she loved me. Due largely to both her lack of enthusiasm and my failure to let a sleeping dog lie (more on this in a later chapter), our relationship died a very slow, agonizing death. Therefore, on the day of the picnic my mood was somber and reflective. I'm sure many of you can relate to the gnawing sense of numbness that tends to overwhelm you when someone who had been a vital part of your life is suddenly not there any more. I felt that in one sense I was there at the picnic, but in another sense I was not. Physically, there I was intermingling with the people around me while my mind was somewhere else entirely. Looking back, I consider that day in the park my very own version of an out-of-body experience. Feeling very detached and objectively observing the couples there was a very eye-opening experience.

To my left there stood a small group of people laughing and talking around a barbecue grill. On the edge of the crowd stood Tameka. Tameka was a tall, slender 23-year old with beautiful doe-like eyes. To many of us there, it was well known that Tameka had a serious thing for John. Her crush was so obvious you would have thought that everyone knew. Everyone that is, except John. John was a very out-going 31-year old in the upper management department. Because of his likable personality, John always had a crowd around him. Male or female, it didn't matter, everybody loved John. Needlessly to say, that day in the park during the picnic was no exception to the rule. John would often with the hordes of women that approached him, he was still unable to find someone he could really connect with. Throughout the picnic it was almost embarrassingly funny how Tameka would make little excuses to keep crossing John's path asking everyone in the crowd (except John) if she could serve them anything. Tameka was trying everything she could to get John to notice her. However, despite all her efforts it was of no use. John's attention was being totally captured by the more aggressive ladies within the usual crowd of people he always seemed to attract. The ironic thing about all this is that John missed a chance to really connect with a lady who could very well have been right for him because he was so used to accepting the attention of women who offered it to him more aggressively. He was unable, or more maybe unwilling to leave his comfort zone of always being the chosen one rather than stepping out and doing some choosing of his own. In this situation, Tameka's shyness definitely worked against her.

To my far right, I noticed that the action was getting hot and heavy at the volleyball net. And I am not talking about the game. I saw Vivian, my friend Henry's wife, standing over in the crowd of spectators holding her dog "Mister" by the leash.

"Who's winning?" I asked. To my surprise she immediately gave me the stats on everything but the game. She pointed out the fact that Darlene, the captain of team-blue with the shape of a super model, was unmistakably making eyes at George. George was the spectacled, slightly balding guy who was standing directly in front of her on team-red. As they faced each other across the net, Darlene never missed a chance to jiggle her breasts or wiggle her butt under the pretense of extra "hustling" to make the big plays. Poor George was certainly catching an eyeful. In fact, it was hard for everybody to keep their attention on the game with the semi-erotic exhibition Darlene was putting on. She was gorgeous. It was obvious how distracted George was. I had never seen him miss as many easy points as he did that day. However, behind Darlene, watching the whole thing was some tall guy with the most angry look on his face I had seen in a long time. I had never seen him before so I asked Vivian who he was and what's his problem. Vivian quickly told me he was Jeff, Darlene's boyfriend. It seemed the two of them had one hell of a heated argument last night. Because of this, Darlene was on a mission to get back at him by making him jealous by flirting with George, whom she actually cared nothing about. She probably only picked George because he happened to be her opposing player in the volleyball game. But George really liked Darlene and he thought opportunity was knocking and this was his lucky day. Sadly, the opposite was true. He had just become the perfect example of someone being in the wrong place at the wrong time. For after the game was over, I watched George as he approached Darlene to see if he had in fact read her clues correctly and she was indeed interested in hooking up after the picnic. It was almost unbearably embarrassing and disheartening to even those of us who were only watching from the sidelines to see how coldly he was snubbed by Darlene. She was using him to make Jeff jealous. You see, she was only flirting with George because she had a use for him. The minute his usefulness was finished, so was he. In her mind, at least. No doubt, she had gotten her flirt on. She had his hopes up because she really led him on. She could have led him anywhere. Unluckily for George, the road led to nowhere, fast. A dead end.

Shortly afterwards, the sun began to set, and we all decided that this was as good a time as any to leave. Vivian, Mister, and I started heading for the parked cars about a hundred yards or so from where we had been standing. On the way out we ran into Zack, a good friend of mine. In the distance I couldn't help but notice the strikingly attractive young lady who was standing there waiting for him by his car. I said to him "Hey, is that the same girl I saw you with last month at the movies that you were so crazy about?" and he said "Nope. I'm afraid not, partner. I tried to get something serious going with her but it didn't work out. You know how it is. I thought she was the one, but I guess I was wrong so the hunt is still on." Just then, Vivian's dog broke away from her and dashed toward a female dog in the parking lot. We laughed as we saw how they circled each other, looked each other over, sniffed each other, and then immediately began to assume that position that dogs made so popular that we had to name it after them. Fortunately, before they managed to really get into it we were able to pull them apart. As we were helping an exasperated Vivian get Mister into the car I looked at Zack and said, "It seems to me like the dogs have it all figured out! They don't have to go thru trial and error. They don't have to go thru a bunch of changes to find the right one for them, like we do. Its all instinct!" Zack replied, "Yeah, maybe we ought to be paying attention. Maybe they're trying to tell us something!" I said, "You know, you might be right." People have been trying everything they know how to get that perfect love hook-up. We've tried this style and that style. We've tried old-school style an even love American style. None of it has been hitting on much so far. Maybe it is time we tried a new style. Maybe its time we tried it DOGGIESTYLE!

Chapter 1
What is a Dog?

What is a dog? Guys, have women ever told you that you were too much of a dog to settle down? Ladies, have guys ever referred to you as that bitch who cheated on them? Perhaps sometimes you weren't even the subject of these derogatory comments. Perhaps you may have only been an innocent by stander when you heard these statements being made by a friend, a relative, or a co-worker. Or maybe the person you most recently heard say these things was you. Have you ever really wondered what in fact calling someone a dog really means? Well, let's define a few terms. If you're one of those people who think that a dog is one of any large group of domesticated, four-legged animals that people choose as pets, you're wrong. Somebody must have slipped you the wrong dictionary. Everybody knows that a dog is a disparaging word used in reference to the opposite sex whenever they are found guilty of committing one love crime or another. For our purposes, the word dog is defined as that part, or that element within all of us totally motivated by the gratification of our own selfish desires. It habitually goes into effect without any moral or ethical considerations towards the feelings of others. The "dog" represents that part of us that only concerns itself with satisfying our basic physical, sensual, or sexual appetites. It usually asserts itself separately from intellectual or spiritual influence. It's the animal influence in every human being, male or female. Psychiatrists call it the ID. The Bible calls it the manifestation of the fallen state of all humanity apart from God because of the sin committed in the Garden of Eden. In other words, it is human nature running wild when it has broken free from the nature of the Divine. However, if you find these definitions too deep or long-winded, you can always call it exactly what it is --- Pure Animal Instinct. Or, as George Clinton used to call it in the Eighties. " It's Just The Dog In You!"

Beware of Dog

Accept it. The reality of The Dog is all around us. But just like AA or any other twelve step program, our first steps to taming the Dog in us all is to first admit we have a problem. Although the hope of living in a world where people choose to be servants to their ideals rather then slaves to their desires is what gives us sweet dreams at night, the reality of how people seek to inconsiderately force their will upon us is the nightmare we live most often. We all have this in common. No one is exempt from the impulse that makes us strive for the things we want with an aggression that has no regard for the feelings of others. The Dog in you can be your best friend sometimes, or it can turn on you and bite you like your worst enemy. The trick to taming your Dog is knowing when to leash it and unleash it. There are times in life when letting the Dog out is good and proper. Those times occur when you need that extra amount of assertiveness that it takes to find and keep a mate. But, there are also times that letting the Dog out is tantamount to self-sabotage. These times occur when you have already found someone with whom you can build a lasting relationship, but you feel strangely dissatisfied. The Dog in you becomes restless. Your eyes start roving. You miss the challenge that was so much a part of your courtship dance. So rather than putting your energies and creative juices into keeping your relationship fresh, you choose the opposite path. Instead, you recklessly throw away your mental, physical, and emotional involvement with your special person like a dog discards his old chew-toy. You get rid of who you've got to go hunt for someone new. Does this behavior sound familiar? If you're guilty of having done this to someone, congratulations! The Dog in you definitely got the best of you. You've been tricked into entering a vicious cycle of self-sabotage that is the main characteristic of being a Hunting Dog (more on that in the next chapter). However, if someone has done this to you and you want to take steps to never let it happen again, hold on because help is on the way!

It's A Dog Eat Dog World

You've heard the saying that it's a dog eat dog world, but do you realize just how true a statement that really is? We live in a Dogmatic society. But before we can manage to learn the art of throwing and fetching equally, let's first expand the picture of the anatomy of a Dog. We do this by primarily recognizing the way in which the Dog in each of us manifests.

Doggietales: Stan, 28

Look, I'm sorry. I gotta have it! I've been with my girl Janice for almost three years now. I know she wants to get married, but hey, I ain't ready yet. I mean, I thought I was ready until I got this new job as a courier. On one of my routes everyday I deliver to this office just full of women. Whenever I bring them their packages, they all line up to flirt with me. It's not anything that I encourage. I guess they can't help it. I may be getting a little older but I keep in shape. I hit the gym five days a week. So I can't really blame them, you know. Whenever one of them compliments me on how good I look, or how muscular my legs are in the uniform that I wear, I take it as an invitation. Even if they're bluffing I feel like I've got to call them on it. I'm a man, you know. If they're with it just for the sex of it, then I'm down with it too! I mean, I love Janice and all, but I gots to get mine! I keep telling her I will marry her someday, but right now it's all about me. I'm having fun. What she doesn't know won't hurt her.

Stan is the classic, almost quintessential, dog that we hear so much about from the ladies that are involved with men like him. For Stan, a one on one relationship is much too boring. His massive ego can only be stroked by the hands of many different women, not just one. Nevertheless, the Doggietales don't just begin and end with Stan, or any other man for that matter. Doggietales are not gender specific. In all fairness, I must remind you that there is a name for female dogs, you know.

Bitches
A bitch is, of course, a name some use to call female dogs. But no matter what you call them, the fact that their bite is just as vicious as any of their male counterparts can't be denied.

Doggietales: Kori, 25
He called me a bitch when I quit him, but that's cool. I guess everybody has a right to their opinion. True, he was nice, but he was too nice. He couldn't make any decisions on his own. Whatever I wanted to do was fine with him. Wherever I wanted to go he would always take me. I could never make him mad enough to even have a good argument. It's stuff like that that used to work my last nerve. I didn't want to be with him! I just couldn't stand that! He just turned me off. What I want is someone who can put his foot down. Someone who's not gonna wait by the phone for me to call him. Someone who won't

always put up with my mess! Someone who'll stand up to me and won't let me run over them. Someone I can't always get my way with so easily. Guys who are too nice, it's not that I treat'em badly, it's just that I can't stand being with them for long. They seem so weak to me. And I can't stand a weak man!

People think I must want a dog. Or someone who will hit me or cheat on me. But that's not it at all. You can call them dogs if you want to, but at least those type of guys are exciting. You never know if they're going to call you when they said they would. You never know if they're going to be on time or stand you up. With a dog, at least you've got some drama and some passion in your life. That's the kind of guy I want. I need somebody who'll l keep me guessing. I need a challenge. And if you can't give me one, I won't stay interested in you for long.

As you can see, Kori is a very opinionated lady. Her outlook on relationships, and how she feels they should work, is very succinct. She's a passion-freak who's into relationships more for the contest than she is for the contentment. So there you have it, two concrete, if not slightly stereotypical examples of real people living in today's Dogmatic society. Both of them indicative of how some people don't walk their dogs, but are instead walked by their dogs.

Who's the master here? Everyone reading should know from now on that when you meet someone interesting and everything's going fine, always keep an eye out for a sign that says BEWARE OF DOG!

Do not take offense with the notion of calling people "Dog". It is the purpose of this book to use the term "Dog" as a metaphor to symbolize the way we all act sometimes in relationships. For at least a decade now we have used the word "Dog" to label both the people we love and the people we love to hate. For example, how many times have you heard the greeting, "What's up, dog?" being said by one friend to another? In our society, we are not strangers to the idea of identifying ourselves with different people, things, and animals in order to make suitable comparisons. How many times have you heard women describe themselves as being attractive "like" Tyra

Banks? How many times have you heard a linebacker hitting the quarterback on a football field "like" a truck?   Lastly, when you consider the multitude of animal names that we have chosen to call many of our pro sports teams such as the Atlanta Falcons and the Chicago Bulls, then the point is made.   Therefore, recognize that "Dog" is only meant to be a good-natured, colloquial term used to illustrate how we sometimes act. Also, know that "Doggiestyle" is a humorous framing device that will hopefully prove very useful to you in helping you tame your lover's doggish ways and allowing you to become the Top Dog in the relationship.

Chapter 2
Ten Types of Dogs: A Visit To The Kennel!

Now that we know what a dog is, now that we know that each of us has a dog in us, let's be more specific. There are many dogs with many names with many characteristics. But in the interest of clarity, we are only going to focus on the ten most prominent types. These are the types that we all will recognize if we are willing to open our eyes. This list is universal. These are people that you meet when you're walking down the street. Yes, these are the people in your neighborhood!

The Ten Types of Dog

1. Hunting Dogs
2. Junkyard Dogs
3. Attack Dogs
4. Show Dogs
5. Tied Dogs
6. Under Dogs
7. Rabid Dogs
8. Dumb Dogs
9. Hot Dogs
10. Top Dogs

Hunting Dogs

Hunting dogs are dogs who like to hunt. They're always looking for somewhere else to bury their bones, so to speak. These type of people are everywhere you look. Hunting dogs is a name that represents those men and women who are addicted to conquest. They are very challenge oriented. The more elusive the prey, the stronger their desire is to hunt. In guys, as a rule, this kind of behavior is very overt. They're very easy to spot. His domain is anywhere an eligible lady can be found. He prowls the city streets, the office buildings, the schoolyards, the church grounds, the night clubs, and anywhere else his endless hunt will take him. We could go on and on naming his various hunting grounds, but you get the point. He's the one you see invading the personal space of every lady unlucky enough to be cornered by his approach.

Sometimes this type of guy comes at you head on. Other times he chooses to sneak up on you from behind. But no matter which way he decides to come at you, rest assured that he is on his way. This is what he does. In fact, this may be all he does.

Male Hunting Dogs have no particular look about them that you can recognize from across a crowded room that will warn of their impending approach. A lot of times the only way you will discover you are both in the presence, and have become the prey of a Hunting Dog is when he speaks. Smooth ain't the word. These guys definitely have the gift of gab and can't wait to bestow it on the next girl they see.

A master conversationalist is the only way you can describe a man who can somehow magically transform a trivial comment into a delightfully engaging topic. A Hunting Dog guy can talk you out of your car, your house, your money, and even your panties. Especially your panties! Unsuspecting ladies fall prey to this type of guy quite often because he's so relaxed, confident, and smooth around them in the things he says and does. This is what they like about him. It rarely occurs to these women in time enough to avoid a heartbreak that the reason why these guys are so sure of themselves around women is because they have had so much practice. Making the acquaintance of a variety of women on a day to day basis is much more than a hobby for them, it's their passion.

Doggietales: Jarrod, age 33

    I've been called a dog before, but to be honest, I don't really Know what that means. When I took this job as an aerobics instructor at the spa, it turned out this job was everything I hoped it was going to be. Ladies everywhere! I mean, it's like a parade in spandex! You know what I'm saying? Ladies of all races, shapes, and sizes dressed in tight colorful leotards that leave nothing to the imagination. Wouldn't you like going to work everyday if you were a young single man like me? Damn right you would! What I like to do is pick one out of the class every now and then and give her a little one on one instruction session. That way I can slowly get closer to her and make her feel like I like her better than the rest. Before too long she feels comfortable enough to start going out with me, and you know what happens next. After we hook up and I hit it a few times, the thrill is gone. But that's all good though, because by that time I've already got my eye on several other ladies at the spa. So before you know it, she's been replaced with the next flavor. I like to call it my Network Principle. What I do when I'm at the spa is throw out a lot of suggestive small talk like a net until it covers the place. Then, when I get three or four nibbles, I'll pull the net in and see which one of'em is really taking the bait. That's how I work it!

As you can see, Jarrod's expertise in "sweating" the babes, so to speak, does not come by happenstance. Instead, from his story, you can tell that he has put quite a lot of thought into the process. Remarkably, he even has a name for what he does. He calls it his Network Principle. Don't sleep on the fact that it's usually a safe bet that no one goes to the trouble of proudly naming a romance technique unless it's successful.

Female Hunting Dogs are usually nowhere near as obvious as the male of the species. They convey their interests in the opposite sex thru mostly subtle ways. Of course there are exceptions to every rule, and in fact there are Hunting Dog females who go after the guys as aggressively as they go after them, but the vast majority of them are much more clever when they are hunting. Hunting Dog girls are everywhere just like the guys also. The difference is, rather than straightforwardly hunting you, they entice you into believing that you are hunting them instead. Why so sneaky? The answer is that they never want to come right out and tell you that they are interested in you because they always want to give themselves enough leeway for deniability in case they suddenly decide they don't want you after all. This way, if you don't measure up for some reason or another, they can always say that you approached them instead of them having approached you.

Hunting Dog girls are thrillseekers. They are looking for nothing more than a quick ego stroke most of the time. If they don't have some man chasing them, begging them, or catering to them 24 hours a day, they think something is wrong. If they have not successfully captured the attention of the most eligible man in the place as soon as they hit party, then they won't leave until they do. You see, it's not enough that they already have a man. It"s that they have to have ALL the men. Hunting Dog girls are incurable flirts. Guys, they're the ones you see at restaurants constantly getting up to walk past your table in particular to make many needless visits to the restroom, bar, or telephone. She's the one who's wearing the jeans so tight that she has to keep standing up at her table just so she can reach into her pocket. The fact that every time she does it all men's eyes are on her is just a coincidence I'm sure. At the trendiest nightclubs she'll be the one on the dance floor dancing just a little freakier than most. Which, by the way, is a hell of a feat to accomplish these days. Why does she premeditatedly entice so many men to rush to her side all at once? That's an easy question with an even easier answer: She needs all the help she can get to hold up that massive ego of hers!

Doggietales: Regina, age 28

Me and my girlfriends were at the restaurant last Saturday night. There were three separate tables full of guys all around us. I had already gotten a couple of phone numbers from the guys at the other tables earlier when we first came in. But this guy at the table in front of us was hot like fire! He was wearing these nice black jeans and this big white sweatshirt. He looked very preppy, which was just my type. The second he walked in I made eye contact with him. I was doing some fierce flirting. When he smiled, I mouthed hello to him from a distance. Because I knew he was looking, I kept thinking of reasons to get up and use the pay phone by his table. I was wearing my low cut body shirt and my favorite pair of jeans that make my butt look just right. It didn't take me but two trips before he asked me for my number. I didn't give him mine, you know. I just took his. I had enough numbers to have enough dates on the weekends to last me the rest of this month. I just took his because I might want to get with him later on. You never know when you might need an extra guy to take you out, right?

As made evident by her story, Regina is an accomplished huntress by any standards. In contrast with Hunting Dog males, the females tend to concentrate on hunting for the future rather than just for today.

So there you have it, a brief profile of Hunting Dogs. They are the rovers with the roving eye. Be on the lookout for them!

Junkyard Dogs

Junkyard Dogs are considered trashy or uncouth people. They are totally unsophisticated. Tact is a word that holds no meaning for them. These type of people live their lives by almost none of the rules that we in a civilized society take for granted. A lot of the times when you see them, their appearance is unkempt and so are their possessions. Junkyard Dog is a name that has no application to a person's financial status at all. It is merely a term that describes a unique world view held by a certain group of people who remain completely uninterested in what we consider the appropriate boundaries of respect for other people and their property. Make no mistake, mind you, these people don't think lowly of themselves. They just view the world, and their place in it, differently. This, in and of itself, is not a bad thing. But when they hook up with someone who is not a Junkyard Dog also, that's when the trouble starts. Junkyard Dogs are a paradox, and they can be very difficult to explain. They seem to love themselves on one hand, but are very comfortable in expecting very little out of themselves on the other. It's not that they have no ambitions, it's just that the things that they aspire to are so mundane and common. But alas, what's common to some is not common to all. It was one of these kinds of people that were probably being addressed in conversations that end in statements like, "See, you ain't used to nothing!". So basically a Junkyard Dog is a kind of person who has disrespect for both his things and the things of others.

You see Junkyard Dogs every day you leave home. These are the guys who roll down the street driving a beat up, near-totalled car with a brand new, state of the art sound system. And of course you know that they have it turned up loud enough to shatter windows a hundred miles away! These are the girls who boldly wear the body-hugging catsuits they had on last night at the club to the office the next day! If you want to experience real culture shock, just try living with a Junkyard Dog.

Doggietales: Janice, age 35

I guess I made the mistake a lot of women in their mid-thirties make. My biological clock was ticking so loud at night that I couldn't even sleep for hearing it. It was around that time that I met Kevin. Kevin used to take me out, hang on my every word, and really pay me a lot of attention. We started having sex a lot at his place. Kevin had a nice apartment but it was always dusty and cluttered with a bunch of broken TV and stereo equipment that he kept claiming he was going to fix. It was kind of uncomfortable over there, so we started spending nights more at my place than his. I'm sure you can guess where this is headed. Kevin eventually moved in, and things were fine for awhile. Then he started bringing more of his stuff in that he claimed he really needed to have. Over the course of the next month and a half, my spacious apartment went from palace to pigsty. He just seemed to never really care about anything. His clothes, his appliances, and all his other stuff was scattered all over my place. If that wasn't bad enough, he soon started breaking up and junking my stuff too. But when I gave him my keys and he wrecked my car and never offered to fix it, that's when I decided I had had enough. He had to go. I really liked Kevin, but it was impossible for me to stay with someone who didn't love me enough to respect my things.

Regina learned the hard way that when you lie down with a Junkyard Dog, it's gonna cost you.

Attack Dogs

Attack Dogs are like Hunting Dogs, but crazed! They almost act as if they are possessed or on drugs sometimes. Everything about their pursuit is hyped up to a dangerous level. These are the people who pursue you relentlessly. Attack Dogs chase after you with an unbridled enthusiasm that can scare you or at least make you terribly uneasy. It's hard to tell sometimes whether or not these kinds of people are either harmless or hazardous. A pretty good rule of thumb to go by is how well they can take an emphatic NO and still remain calm and civil in your presence. Alarmingly though, even this is not a failsafe method. Some of these people come from such a place emotionally where they are either so infatuated or needy that the line between fantasy and reality blurs before their eyes. They are not sensible and they are not rational. When they finally see they won't get anywhere with you, they will move on only to go out and find them another target for their claustrophobic attentions. Their behavior is cyclical because they count on each new person they meet to be THE ONE. The Attack Dogs' desperation always proves their undoing.1

These people are no joke. Their desperation drives them into states of mind where they could entertain ideas of being stalkers, rapists, or something much worse.

Doggietales: Craig, age 43

I'll never forget it. I met her when I was attending night school at the university. I knew she was young, but I was just so attracted to her. I was picking up vibes from her that were telling me that she was interested in more than just a platonic relationship. So I thought to myself, what the hell. My divorce is almost final. It's about time for me to get back into the swing of things as far as dating was concerned. Sharonda was as sexy a lady to start with as any. She was also almost 20 years younger than me. I have to admit that it was a major turn-on for me to be out on the town with someone that young and pretty. Things were lovely for about a month or two, but eventually the age differences in our relationship started to show up. The things she liked to do were vastly different from my idea of a good time.

She wasn't happy with quiet, intimate evenings. She was more up for partying all weekend or going to every concert tour that came to town. But all that type of stuff just didn't really appeal to me. I guess all those years of marriage had turned me into a homebody and I kind of like it. Things kept getting worse between me and Sharonda. So I found the guts one day to break it off with her. I tried to explain to her that it was best if I went on with my life and she went on with hers. Her only answer was silence. She just sat there for a moment and then left without saying a word. Then about a week later all hell broke loose. She started calling me and threatening me. She told me to take her back or I was going to be sorry. She said she was in love with me, but I call it obsession. I caught her following me 3 times. She said she was making sure I wasn't dating anyone else. I refused to return her calls. So one night while I was sleep, she came over and spray painted my only car and smashed all my windows. It turned out that the only way I could get her off my back was to put a restraining order on her. If I had known it was going to end like that I never would have dated her. So far, I haven't had anymore drama with Sharonda. But I would be lying if I told you I wasn't still looking over my shoulder expecting to catch her stalking me all over again.

We can all learn a lesson from Craig. Attack Dogs are no laughing matter, and should never be taken lightly. Be careful out there.

Show Dogs
Show Dogs are people who would either like to put on a show or see a show. These folks are unashamedly materialistic. Their preference is style over substance every time. These are the "Dogs" you see chasing cars. The more expensive and flashier the cars, the better. Once again, no one gender can claim sole ownership to either particular facet of the Show Dog personality. Still, historical observation shows us that men seek to impress women more with the things that they've got than the other way around. Meanwhile, Show Dog women seek men

17

whom they perceive as having a lot of things. Admittedly, it can be said that the distinctions between Show Dog men and women are just overused stereotypes. However, there is just enough truth hidden beneath the surface of this typecasting to give it credence.

Show Dog type people come across as either Exhibitionists or Acquisitionists. The Exhibitionist Show Dogs are easily reconizeable because they are seen so frequently. The reason you see them so much is because they're always on parade. Yes, they're putting on a show for everybody to see. They too, like Shakespeare, believe that all the world is but a stage. They differ from Shakespeare radically though in the sentiment that we are all merely players. The way Show dogs see it is that anybody can be a player, they would rather be the stars! Folks who run in this pack subscribe to the idea that they must always shine brighter than everybody else. They find no rationale in using things and loving people. They would much rather stick to loving things and using people. Their sense of self worth is not self worth at all. It's about material worth only. It's all about the Benjamins, baby! They only feel as valuable as the car they drive, the money they make, the house they own, the clothes they wear, or the jewelry they're sporting. Please don't misunderstand, attaining great material possessions isn't at all a bad thing in and of itself. However, when you find your self more proud to show off what you have rather than who you are, you may have a problem. Let's keep it real, we all need money to survive. We all want nice things. The trouble with Show Dogs is that they lead with their style and never follow with their substance. It's hard for them to settle comfortably into a lasting relationship because they can never be sure whether or not the other person loves them for themselves or for their money, status, or perceived power. Again, let's not fool ourselves. Not all these Exhibitionists are looking for love. A lot of them are quite content in taking lovers just to use them as ornaments or accessories to wear on their sleeves. It's not unheard of for them to date certain people solely for the purpose of feeding their public's consumption. If they always have a different, beautiful person on their arm while they're out in public, this only helps to further solidify their superstar status in their own minds.

Doggietales: Ronald, age 41

Last summer was the best. That was when we first started the cable dance show. The show features a lot of local talent as well as big name musical celebrities. It's been almost a year and the show is doing well in the ratings. But just as important as that is how I've been picking up a few extra perks along the way. The ladies are what I'm speaking of. Every week we audition new girls to dance for the show. Since I'm the program producer, they all have to come thru me. It's gotten to be funny in a way. I don't even have to try to go after them anymore because now they're all coming after me. They see me pull up in the parking lot in my cranberry, drop top Jag and I've found that tapping my car horn is all the conversation I need to swing'em my way. Just to drive all the women crazy, every time I show up at the studio I'm wearing a different $600 suit. Listen, I'm making bigger money now, so I make sure I never buy my clothes off the rack anymore. Of course, with every new crop of young ladies that come in, I make sure to mention that I am the program producer every chance I get. See, I know how women are. They all want to get with the money man. So I let'em know it's all about me! After that, my clothes and my cars do the rest. I personally think that women act more like children. In fact, the prettier the women, the more like a child you have to treat them. That's why I love to ride them around in my Jag so they can see what real luxury is. Besides, everybody knows that women are fascinated with bright, shiny things with flashing buttons and knobs. Usually, if I can get them inside my car, they're as good as bagged. They're frozen stiff, like a deer caught in the headlights. And just like a deer, that's when I hit'em.

Now that we've heard a genuine account of the life of a true Exhibitionist Show Dog, let's see what we can learn from it. Two things in particular are worthy of note. Number one is that Ronald knows exactly how to attract women who are drawn primarily to material things. He knows that they love to see a show, so he gladly puts on one for them. Secondly, based on how badly he talked about the women in question, we can easily see that he has a very low opinion of the golddiggers he so loves to impress.

Acquistitionist Show Dogs chase after all the stuff that other people have rather than trying to get their own. They are the perfect match for the Exhibitionist Show Dog. You could say that they deserve each other.

There is nothing more pleasing to a master than to have a ready and willing slave. Willing slavery is not too harsh a way to describe the way Acquisitionist Show Dogs carry on. They are drawn to the appearance of money and power just like a moth is drawn to a flame. Unfortunately, much to their chagrin, this category of people make the mistake of throwing themselves at people they consider to be walking goldmines. Imagine their surprise on those occasions when they find out that the person they were after who had the appearance of money and power has only that. No money or power at all, just the appearance of it. Egads! Another bank robber foiled again!

It's a shame, but you can't always know these Acquisitionist Show Dogs by their outward appearance. The reason why is because the irony of the situation is that even though they value material things highly, they don't usually have many things themselves. As a result, they choose to concentrate on augmenting their attitudes and physical appearances instead. They use what they've got to get what they want. Unlike the Hunting Dog mentioned earlier, these types are much more specific about the kind of person they're looking for. Money reigns supreme over almost everything. They have a stronger need to be rescued than they have to be self-sufficient. After all, why should they work when they can get you to work for them? They're more than happy to be thought of as just another trophy for their suitors to show off. It's not enough that you have money, clothes, a car and a job to get the attention of these types of people. Instead, you'd better make sure you have enough money, the right clothes, the right car, and the right job to pique their interests.

Doggietales: Joyce, age 25

    I met this guy last weekend. He came into the grocery store where I work and did a lot of shopping. He looked to be in his mid-thirties. He had on a tailor-made suit and some really expensive eyeglasses. While he was standing in line, he struck up a conversation with me. I could tell by the things he said and the way he carried himself that he was very highly educated.

21

When he paid for his groceries and prepared to leave, he turned and asked if we could get better acquainted. I said yes and he gave me his business card. I read his card and was very disappointed by what I saw. He wasn't a doctor or a lawyer or anything like I thought. He was only an insurance agent. No matter how hard I try, it's just hard for me to see myself with an insurance salesman. I was expecting much more than what I got. I can't really put my heart into dating a man if I'm not impressed by what he does for a living. So I never called him.

Well, Joyce's story is not unusual in today's dating world. She represents the kind of person who has to like the man's job before she will even consider him a viable candidate for a relationship. There was no denying that she was turned on by his looks, personality, and his conversation. But all this became null and void once she found his occupation wanting. So Joyce chose to slam the door on a possible successful relationship simply because she had a condescending attitude about what the guy does for a living. She's really looking for finance, not romance. So the next time you meet an Acquisitionist Show Dog and you are tempted to ask how much is that doggie in the window gonna cost you. Realize that if you have to ask, you probably can't afford it.

Tied Dogs
Tied Dogs are just what the name implies. They are people with ties. To avoid any confusion, we're not talking about people who have neckties. Instead we're talking about people who have ties that bind them to other people. They're already in relationships. They can be married, living together, or simply seriously involved with someone else. However, they seldom miss a chance to bury their bones in new places. Tied Dogs don't seem to understand the concept of making a choice. Even though they'll be glad to fool around with you too, they never forget that they have ties to someone else and will almost never leave them for you. Why should they? Why should they make a choice when they can comfortably enjoy the fruits of a primary

and a secondary relationship? They justify their behavior by telling themselves that each lover has something that the other doesn't. This rationalizing affords them an easy excuse for not taking responsibility for possibly causing pain to all those involved. They have a selfishness that is akin to greed. Everything they see, they want. They want their share and yours too. Already having their fair share doesn't quench their thirst to taste other flavors of the opposite sex that they encounter.

In an effort to stay in dating circulation, Tied Dogs often masquerade as being untied. Some of them play the role of a single person so well, that they actually take on a whole other identity. These impostors are so convincing sometimes that it could take a gullible or unsuspecting person months to figure out they're really married with children!!

Doggietales: Monica, age 23

I've been going out with Montel for about 7 months now. I met him while I was attending graduate school. He was the guess speaker at a seminar that we were required to attend. He was fascinating to watch up there on the podium. I felt an attraction for him immediately. He had slightly gray hair and looked very distinguished. He was suave and sophisticated. He was watching me watching him all while he was speaking. Afterwards, he asked me out for a cup of coffee and I quickly agreed. We really seemed to click together so we started dating fairly regularly after that. After a certain amount of times, it began to dawn on me that he had never invited me over to his place. We always met at mine. After I started throwing hints around about my suspicions that something was wrong, he finally invited me over to his apartment. Once there, I began to feel more at ease until I began to notice that his apartment was barely furnished at all. I asked him why this was so and he told me it was because he really didn't need a lot of furniture because he was traveling doing seminars all the time. As time went by, he even went so far as to giving me a set of keys to his apartment. Then, just as I was about to dismiss all my suspicions as me just being paranoid, I got the shock of my life one day when I answered his phone and his wife called! You see, Montel was married. He just happened to meet me during his separation. Most of the time he claimed to be out of town lecturing, he was really trying to get back into the good graces of his wife. The day I answered his phone was the day his wife was calling to find out when he was officially going to move back in with her! You could imagine how devastated I was. He never wore a wedding band. And whenever I asked him if he was married or seeing anybody else, he always said he wasn't. It turns out that he was only using me as his standby woman just in case his wife didn't take his ass back.

Monica had the misfortune of falling for a very well disguised Tied Dog and was badly bitten. Although the bite will leave a scar, it will also serve as a constant reminder of something she could have done to avoid the situation entirely. Monica should have paid less attention to her emotions and more attention the the vibes she was picking up all along. She should have asked more questions than she did. One good way to sniff out whether or not you're dealing with a Tied Dog masquerading as an untied one is to ask probing questions when the timing is appropriate. Anyone who has a problem answering a straightforward question has something to hide. Also, if the answers that are given sound a little too made up, it's usually because they are.

Doggietales: Jerry, age 27

I'll never do it again. I can promise you that! Miranda was the kind of lady that as soon as you see her enter the room, every other lady disappears. I remember it very clearly. I was at a hotel party this past Christmas when I first saw her sitting at a table with 5 other women. I had arrived at the party a little late so I couldn't get a table so I did what every guy does in a situation like that. I found me a spot on the wall and got comfortable. You see, some people don't realize that standing against the wall serves two purposes. First, it gives you high visibility so that all the women can check you out as they go by. Secondly, and more importantly to me, standing on the wall gives you the best view of all the ladies as they go by and you won't have worry about missing any of them. Anyway, so I'm standing there posin' 'til closin' when Miranda catches my eye. I couldn't help myself. I was scoping her out the whole night. As the music kept pumping, I checked out how out of all the women at the table, only Miranda carried herself like a lady. Most of the other women at the table were much louder and wilder. In my mind, Miranda somehow seemed to act as if she were above it all. Not in a snobbish way did she carry herself, but with a maturity you would expect from a much older woman. Over time, I saw she was giving me the eye just like I was giving it to her. I finally approached her and gave her my number. She took mine, but never gave me hers. She claimed she wanted to get to know me better. The next month was like a dream to me. Miranda was everything I ever fantasized about in a lady. We shared so many things in common, like loving old movies, listening to all that great music from the eighties, and even stuff as silly as a preference for a double-cheese pizza. As you can tell, I was either in love or damn near. Even though most of the time we spent together was at my house, in my mind we were together so often that it never dawned on me that I had never been to hers. One day before I could even bring the subject up, she dropped a bomb on me. She came to me and flat out told me she was living with a guy. They had been together for five years, and lived together for three of them. She told me that she liked me a lot, but loved him. It seems that his job called for him to travel out of town for months at a time. She said all she was really looking for was a part-time friend, not a full-time love affair. She had no problems continuing to have sex just as long as I understood that when her live-in guy came to town he would be her number one priority. Well, I'm ashamed to say that for six months I swallowed my pride, my morals, and I guess everything else that was important to me just to be with her whenever I could. After awhile though, being her secret lover started hurting so bad that I finally got the guts to break it off with her for good. Now, even though it's been over for about two months, I still get booty calls from her when I least expect them. So far, I've been able to stay strong and stay away. Even though I know it's stupid to hook up with a girl I can never have just for me, it still ain't easy.

Poor Jerry was on the receiving end of a bad experience. Miranda kept throwing frivolities at him, but he kept catching feelings. During his interview, Jerry kept swearing up and down that he would never again let himself fall for someone who was emotionally off limits to him. Let's hope he keeps his promise and remains a man of his word.

Lastly, there are some Tied Dogs who don't masquerade at all. These characters are so confident in their ability to attract the kinds of people they want they they don't even bother trying to hide their involved status.

Doggietales: Janet, age 33

Yes, I know he's married. I've been in a relationship with him for five years, so of course I know he's married. Michael is a police officer that I met the day he pulled me over for driving with suspended tags. Instead of just writing me a ticket, he said he'd let me off with a warning if I would have lunch with him the next day. True, he might have been just joking when he said it, but I took him seriously. So I accepted his offer. Something about a man in a uniform always does it for me. Over the next few weeks, our lunches turned to dinners, and our dinners turned into weekend trysts where we never got out of bed. I didn't know then that I was going to fall in love with him, but I guess it just happened. He's been having a lot of trouble with his wife, lately. He told me that if it wasn't for his four kids, he would have left her a long time ago. We're still seeing each other, and I know he loves me because he told me so. I know that if I just hang on, she'll make that one last mistake that will give him enough of an excuse to finally leave her. That's when we'll finally be together. When that day comes, we won't have to hide anymore. I've got friends that tell me there are much too many single guys out there for me to be spending my time with with a married one. In my opinion though, men are all the same. I've always thought that you have your best chance for a long-standing relationship with a married man anyway. I mean, when you really think about it, at least they know something about commitment.

As strange as it may seem, Janet's statement might actually have some truth to it. Married men who act like Tied Dogs do indeed know something about commitment: They know what it is NOT.

Under Dogs
Some could argue that Under Dogs aren't even dogs at all. In fact, they act more like whipped puppies. Their sense of self-worth is not yet full grown. These hapless individuals are overly kind, docile people. This kindness is frequently taken for weakness by more aggressive folks. These stronger willed folks generally find Under Dogs uninteresting.

In our society, Under Dogs represent that segment that are considered Yes-men and Yes-women. They give up their freewill in order to submit to the will of others. These poor people have sadly either forgotten they have a backbone, or have temporarily forgotten how to use it. Although it only has one syllable, the word "no" is very hard for them to pronounce. What we think of ourselves is a direct result of how we have dealt with the positives and negatives of our pasts. Reaching for higher levels of confidence is quite a stretch for an Under Dog kind of person. That's because confidence is often the result of vivid memories of our past successes. Naturally, it seems to follow that if an Under Dog's success in relationships is elusive, it may largely be because their self-confidence also is fugitive.

People who are classified as Under Dogs, though they may be eager to have good relationships, sometimes unknowingly project how badly they feel about themselves to others. Subconsciously, they set in motion chains of events that bring to life their worst fears of being dogged out. How a person behaves and allows him or herself to be treated reveals what they really think of themselves. It's all a matter of perception. Under Dogs are people of whom this quote would apply, "I wouldn't wanna belong to any club that would have me as a member!" Enough

27

hard life lessons can force us into being more assertive in our relationship styles. It's not necessary to be the one in total control in a relationship, just as long as you're not always the one taking orders and acquiescing at every turn. Nobody can long survive in a relationship where they are the giver who never gets. Nobody can pretend forever that being treated like a doormat is fun or even acceptable. It's amazing though, how so many people with whipped puppy mentalities seem to go for overly aggressive or overbearingly pushy lovers. They are like slaves in search of masters. They appear to the casual onlooker as gluttons for punishment. They are the sort of people who pretend to overlook things that hurt their feelings. Even when their lovers do things toward them that are grossly inconsiderate, Under Dogs never call them on it. For them, nothing is worth risking irritating their lover. No matter how condescending or abusive the act, they would rather martyr their self-respect than possibly lose their relationship.

If you are much too eager to please, or give in too much too often, you are destined to be thought of as a non-person in any new relationship. In addition, by masquerading as someone other than who you really are, you'll only succeed in attracting somebody who's only attracted to who you're pretending to be. Whenever you do find the courage to be yourself, the object of your affection will feel betrayed and disappointed because you're not the person your were pretending to be. By hiding who they really are, Under Dogs usually only end up wasting their time trying to keep someone around they're probably incompatible with anyway.

Conducting their love lives in this fashion can even cost Under Dogs relationships with people they really are compatible with. When Under Dogs bite their tongues all the time, they are teaching the people they're with that anything goes. Closed mouths never get fed. By being tight-lipped about what they really want out of a relationship, they are teaching their lovers that whatever they are presently doing is all good and should continue. Let's be honest about the dog in us. That aggressive part of human nature is often kept under control because people fear the possibility of retaliation coming from the person who has been aggressed upon. In our society, being too forceful or too aggressive can get you in a lot of trouble. People are arrested all the time for being uncontrollably aggressive. Most considerate people don't yearn to be bullies. But when Under Dogs never express an opinion, it's human nature for the more decisive lover to take over. By letting themselves be run over all the time, Under Dogs take away all the negative consequences that are ordinarily linked to overly aggressive behavior. People only dog out Under Dogs because they allow it.

Doggietales: Donna, age 36:

My first marriage ended in divorce. I don't really know what happened, but I guess it was my fault. I tried to do everything just the way my first husband wanted it. First, I quit my interior decorating career so I could have more time for him. Then, although it took a couple of years, I finally became pregnant and gave him the son he wanted. Just a few years after Ryan was born, my first husband started to shut me out. He grew more and more distant. Then one day he told me he didn't love me anymore and wanted to be free. Maybe there was something I could have done, but I decided it was probably best for the kids that I not put up a big fight. So I let the marriage end. That was 9 years ago, now I'm dating Chris. When I first met him, I didn't know he was married. But by the time I did find out, I was too much in love with him to let him go. I don't really see anything wrong with it when he tells me what to do. Sure, sometimes I would rather do things I like, but it's a small sacrifice to make for keeping Chris around. He's the best thing that's ever happened to me. I'm a single mother who isn't getting any younger, and Chris may be my last chance at true love.

It's easy to recognize how what Donna thinks of herself is always tied to how the men in her life think of her. As long as she continues to let things remain this way, her love life may forever be a tangled mess. Sometimes, the best thing that Under Dogs can do to change their ways is to act totally the opposite of how they usually do. Just long enough to see how it feels to have confidence for a change. If they will only decide to exercise their confidence little by little, over a period of time they will be surprised to discover how strong their sense of self-worth can become.

Rabid Dogs

Rabid Dogs are exactly what the name implies. Rabid Dogs are people infected with pain and resentment from past relationships. We all know that in the animal world, rabies is an infectious disease closely associated with canines. In humanity, rabies is another way of defining the condition that some people suffer from who have been badly hurt or damaged by their relationships with others. Rabies in human beings can be diagnosed just by taking a look at the amount of emotional baggage that a person carries with them into a new relationship from a previous one. Rabid Dog men and women are the type of people who go out looking for new love before they've gotten over the old one.

If you meet a Rabid Dog person, you'll know them by how they act. They are the finger-pointers, the name-callers, and the blame-game players that are infecting the world all around us. They lack a certain amount of maturity because they refuse to take any responsibility for the outcome of their last relationship. It's always easier to blame the other person completely. They walk around with a chip on their shoulder that's sometimes big enough to see from a distance. They are the prophets of doom. They are so pessimistic about love because they're still in shock from their last failed romance. Before they even meet you, they've already decided that any new relationship will end in ruin.

Doggietales: Carly, age 35

Elton was the brother of a friend of mine at work. I guess you can call Ellen my best friend. I'd known her for years, and she knew all the details about my private life. She knew all about how rocky my marriage to my then husband Riley had been. I tried to hang in there with him, but Riley had a habit that used to work my last nerve. Riley's problem was that he was chronically late. It didn't matter what the occasion or the event was, he would always be late. It didn't matter if it was something concerning me, him, or the kids, he never thought enough of it to be on time. It had to actually be a life or death situation for him to be on time for something. That may sound sad, but I think it's really true. I finally filed for divorce because I felt like his lateness showed that he really didn't think enough of me to be more considerate towards me. Months after my divorce was final, Ellen decided to hook me up with her brother. I'd met Elton on a few occasions already, so I decided to give him a shot. Elton and I had many long, enjoyable, phone conversations for a week and a half before we scheduled a date. I was impressed by his intelligence and the fact that he wasn't as shallow as some other guys. We set a date for Saturday night at 7:00 p.m. I had just gotten my hair and nails done and was very excited about going out with him. I sat by the window and nervously waited for him. Seven o'clock turned to eight o'clock. I was furious by the time eight o'clock turned to eight-thirty. So furious in fact, that I called and left a message for him on his answering machine. I don't know exactly what I said, but I do remember cursing like a sailor and calling him every name in the book! I do remember telling him at the end of the call that he was just as inconsiderate as my ex-husband and to never call me again. That following Monday at work, I could barely look Ellen in the eye. She took the lead and approached me first. She told me that Saturday night, on the way to my place, Elton was in a bad car wreck. He got away lucky with only a broken leg and a mild concussion. It seems that he was going to call me and tell me about it on Sunday, but once he got my answering machine message he changed his mind. He sent word by Ellen that there was no way he was going to date a woman with mood swings as crazy as mine. After she told me this, the only thing that ran thru my mind was how this was all Riley's fault. He's the reason why I act the way I do.

Though she finds it hard to believe, Carly's position is not a unique one. True, Carly was betrayed by Riley constantly letting her down, but she's not the only person who's ever been in a

31

predicament like this. Although she had every right to hold him liable for dogging her out in the past, she should have recognized that Elton was a whole new person with a whole new set of circumstances. No way he was responsible for the wounds inflicted on her by that buster she used to be with. Nor should he have been made to pay the price for pain she had in the past. Carly is like that psycho-mom in the neighborhood who whips all three of her kids when only one of them broke her favorite vase! Her warped logic tells her that she's whipping all of them so that they'll know that she's not having that kind of horseplay in her house!

Doggietales: Dennis, age 29

Tamesa was a tough act to follow. But then, I knew she would be. Tamesa was the girl I fantasied about whenever I visualized the ideal woman for me. She had the body of an Amazon. She was looked like Xena on TV. She was luscious. She had the lips, the hips, and all that. I wasn't buying that love at first sight nonsense before I met her. When we first started seeing each other she was very outgoing and passionate. It was hard for me to believe at first that a "monster BABE" like Tamesa could go for me as much as she did. I guess there were little signs that something was wrong along the way, but I chose to ignore them. I tried not to really pay attention to how she always wanted me to buy her something new whenever we were going out on the town. I tried not to notice how moody she was when we had to ride around in my second-hand Nova after my Mazda 323 was wrecked. I also chose to ignore how she managed to max out all the credit cards that I let her borrow. In a way, you can argue that I had my head up my ass during the entire time we were together. However, at the time I didn't care, because I was just so thrilled to have Tamesa. The only thing I couldn't ignore though, was how she flirted with my boss at last year's Christmas party. I tried to tell myself I was blowing things out of proportion. However, when I caught her rubbing his thigh with one hand and slipping him her number with the other, I blew my top! I ended our relationship right there on the spot. I told her she better catch a ride home with him, because she definitely wasn't riding with me! I made up my mind right then that Tamesa was going to be the last woman that I would ever let play me like that. After that, it seemed like every attractive woman was a suspect. I met this girl named Gladys at Freaknic this year. She was an amateur model from Seattle. I got with her for awhile and everything started out cool initially, just like they always do. From the moment I met her, we seemed to relate to each other like we'd known each other for years. She had a good personality, and wasn't hard to look at either. I get the feeling that she may be wanting to get serious about taking our relationship to a more serious level, but I'm not having it. I'm not putting myself in a position to play that sucker role again.

Dennis is the kind of Rabid Dog that suffers from what I'd like to call the X-Filing of Romance. Anyone familiar with network programming is familiar with the X-Files. The X-Files is a TV show that deals with paranormal activity and multiple conspiracy theories. People who are fans of this show are called X-Philes. This is kind of how Dennis is. Just like the fans of that TV show, he fears that everything and everyone he meets is all part of some huge conspiracy. In his mind, they're all out to get him! He's closed the door on all possibilities that anything to the contrary could be true. You see, Rabid dogs are obsessed with X-factors. They're held hostage by the unknown quantities of romantic life. They have convinced themselves that all unknown factors that they encounter are going to only be negative. The reason is because this is what the sum-total of their past experiences have taught them. They're so infected by the bad Dog bites they've received in the past that they have been made rabid. Rather then starting a new relationship, what they really need is time for reflection and reevaluation. In other words, what they really need is a Rabies Shot. Until they get one, and have shown signs of recovery, they should be avoided at all costs.

Dumb Dogs

Dumb Dogs are the funniest dogs in the kennel. Very rarely do they come across as threatening in any way. More often, they are quite upbeat and friendly. If you believe the phrase that says that ignorance is bliss, then it should come as no surprise to you that Dumb Dogs are very, very happy. People who like to think of themselves as intelligent and vastly smarter than others, tend to find Dumb Dogs as a constant source of aggravation and frustration. Dumb Dogs are rebels without a clue. Whenever you meet one, the letters S.O.S. come to mind. Not necessarily because they need help, but because they're Stuck On Stupid. Listen, you wouldn't call these people airheads exactly, but if you were to place a microphone next to their ear you'd definitely hear the sound of a mighty, rushing wind!

Something else about Dumb Dogs you should know is that they proudly display their "dumbness" because they have no inkling of just how dumb they really are. For the benefit of those who live in a state of denial, please answer the following questions:

1. Do you sit around with a blank look on your face and your mouth hanging open until you are snapped out of this state by the sound of someone calling your name to get your attention? Well, then you're probably a Dumb Dog.
2. Have you ever been involved in a car accident where you hit a telephone pole and when the police officer arrived you argued that it wasn't your fault because you blew the horn? Well then, you might be a Dumb Dog.
3. Have you ever been real excited to go to a football game only to be disappointed once you got there when they told you that a Quarterback wasn't a refund? Well, if you haven't guessed it by now, you're definitely a Dumb Dog!

The interesting thing about Dumb Doggietales, is that they are usually told from the point of view of the "smarter" lover.

Why, you might ask? The reason is because nobody alive would ever plead guilty to being dumb without a court order!

Doggietales: Leslie, age 27

My sister Sandra is a court reporter. One Tuesday morning at work she met this guy who came and struck up a conversation with her during one of the recesses. This guy, Michael, was there that day to defend himself against five women who had filed charges against him for swindling them. He was on trial for being an accused Con Man. Sandra told me that she got to know him pretty well over the next couple of weeks while he was standing trial. Actually, she got to know him better than she let on, because I later found out that she was so taken by him that she had asked him to move in with her. He'd told her that he enjoyed being with her, but his finances were drying up because of legal fees. You don't have to be Sherlock Holmes to figure out what happened to her next. Pretty soon, Michael had charged up all Sandra's credit cards, cleaned out her bank account, and then skipped town in her brand new Honda Accord! After that whole episode had run it's course, I asked Sandra what on earth was she thinking dating a Con Man in the first place. But when she answered, she corrected me. She said, "I didn't know he was a Con Man, all I knew was that he was accused!"

What is the best way that we can describe Sandra? Let's just say that all her lights are on, but nobody's home.

Doggietales: Floyd, age 24

I was out at the jazz club the other night at about 8:30 when this drop dead gorgeous girl came in. She was stunning. Her hair, her clothing, her make-up, and everything else about her was impeccable. Things had been dead for about 2 hours before she got there. I stepped to her as soon as I saw her. I wanted to get my bid in before any other guys could. The closer I got to her, the more she began to look familiar. Suddenly, I recognized her as Raechelle, a girl I had been trying to get with for the past two months. In the past, whenever I asked her out, she always had an excuse as to why she couldn't make it. Seeing it was her pissed me off, but I walked over to her table anyway. But, before I could get there, some tall guy took a seat next to her. I said to her, " Hi Raechelle, how are you?" She spoke back, and then tried to introduce me to the guy next to her. I said she "tried to" because she couldn't seem to remember his name, so he introduced himself. She told me that her and this guy met each other over the phone today when she had to call the copy center where he worked in order to place a business order. She said that they felt so comfortable talking to each other earlier that they agreed to meet for drinks after work tonight. I was shocked at how nonchalant she was in telling me this, seeing as how she knew how much I had been trying to get with her. I couldn't help myself . I got so mad I said, "You mean to tell me I've been asking you out all this time and you wouldn't do it, yet you go out on blind dates!?" The guy didn't say anything as Raechelle looked up at me and said, "Blind date? What do you mean a blind date? This isn't a blind date! I don't even know this guy!!!

There are many ways you could categorize Raechelle's state or mind. For now, let's just say she's a few fries short of a happy meal.

Doggietales: Susan, age 34

I'm feeling kind or nervous. I feel kind of uncomfortable about this, but this is so funny that I've got to tell somebody. Last year, before me and Marion got married, we got into this big argument about whether or not I would take his last name or simply add his last name to mine. I remember it as clearly as if it had just happened. I met Marion at the casino he manages right after I had just given my English class it's final exam. In order to get tenure at the university, it's very important that you publish some of your own work. I had already managed to publish 2 essays on Chaucer for the university's press under my maiden name. My concern was that the notoriety that I was beginning to enjoy as a published writer might be obscured by the sudden name change that traditionally comes from being married. I was sharing this with Marion and I assured him that I loved him, but it was just that I was thinking about my career also. I told him we could still be married without us both having the same name. He told me that he was an old-fashioned type guy and he felt that his wife should have the same last name as her husband. He told me that he didn't care what anybody else thought. I replied, "Don't you think you're making much too big a deal out of this? Who cares whether or not we have the same last name, anyway? After all, even the English department's favorite bard Shakespeare himself once said, "What's in a name?" Marion, paused and frowned. He looked at me with a very serious look on his face and said, "I'm the one who loves you! Are you going to listen to me, or are you going to listen to your co-workers!?"

Now that's hilarious! This tale just goes to show you that you should never underestimate the stupidity of a Dumb Dog. Just when you think you've seen and heard it all, they keep coming up with new ways to top themselves!

Hot Dogs

Hot Dogs are raw dogs. They are like a Hunting Dogs with an X-rated attitude. They're the segment of society that is totally indiscriminate. They have no real sense of sexual rights or wrongs. They are dogs in heat. Anytime is the best time, and anyplace is the best place!

They don't just walk their dogs, they run them. The only thing they say in response to their outrageous sexual escapades is that they're only doing what comes natural. More reserved people usually beg to differ. To keep it real, the truth is that they have decided that they would rather be ruled by their five senses than their good senses. Hot Dogs might not necessarily love the people they're with, but they do love the sights, sounds, touches, tastes, and smells of having sex with them though. These men and women spell love L-U-S-T. As one lady in Chicago put it, "I just gotta keep gettin' my freak on!" If the call ever went out for all good men an women to take a vow of sexual abstinence for just 24 hours, Hot Dogs would NEVER answer it. As a matter of fact, the only call Hot Dogs will ever answer is a Booty Call. A Booty Call, of course, is an invitation for sex usually made late at night that is completely casual and has no commitments whatsoever.

Doggietales: Camille, age 21:

Yeah, it's all about a Booty Call. A lot of guys talk about how good they are in bed, but I've only found a few of them who could actually back it up. To be honest, the guy I'm with now is the best I've ever had. I know he's married, but what's that got to do with anything? As long as he can keep coming over 3 or 4 times a week to get with me, I'm satisfied. I've even met his wife a few times and I think she may know about us. Hey, if she wants to cook for him in the day time while he's "cooking" for me at night, that's her business. Like I said, he's the best I've had in a long time and I'm not going to be quick to let him go. It took me almost 11 months before I found someone who could do it as good as he can, so you know I'm not going to blow a good thing. Uhh, so to speak.

Camille has a habit that renders her morally ambiguous. Never once in her quest for the best sex ever did she ever stop to think how the man's wife was suffering from their little nighttime encounter sessions. For her, the married guy she's doing only represents a means to an end. She's got a habit, and the habit is constant sex. Her need to make Booty Calls impairs her judgment just as much as if she were intoxicated on drugs or alcohol.

Diner Sex vs. Drive-Thru sex

Hot Dogs usually have one or two things in mind when they're out looking for company. They are either looking for Diner Sex or Drive-Thru sex. One is cheap, the other is quick, and neither are too good for you.

Diner Sex is the kind of coupling that gives the appearance of a true romantic relationship but has none of the substance. The random acts of romance and caring that take place under the guise of dating is reduced to a mere facade in this kind of situation. These falsified love affairs are perpetuated solely for the purpose of satisfying each participants sexual appetites. In

38

other words, they're only in it to hit it. Sometimes, at least one of the people involved in this type of arrangement is only in it out of boredom or lack of other options. As a result, when either one of them gets a better sex offer, they're out the door. The harshness of leaving the other person hanging is lost on them. Remember, theirs was not a love thing, just a temporary thing.

Contrastingly, Drive-Thru sex is more straightforward and requires very little explanation. This is sex with no expectations, no commitments, no guilt, and no manogomany. Hot Dogs who practice this type of sex are very much into one night stands. It is the preferred type of sexual rendezvous of those who like to hit and run just for fun. It's a one night performance with no plans for a return engagement planned.

There is a distinction between men and women Hot Dogs. For women, sex is a judgment. For men, sex is job. According to the people interviewed for this book, getting sex for a woman is a whole lot easier than it is for a man. If a woman, even a very unremarkable-looking woman, decides she wants to have sex, all she usually has to do is go out and get it. Once she's out on the town flirting and dressed provocatively, she'll almost certainly get a proposition from some guy. Even if she fails to entice the guy she really wants, somebody's going to show some interest!

For men though, it's different. Even if you use the same scenario and let the man be very handsome, getting sex for him will look very much like work. It's just a fact that men, even some good-looking men, have to put in much more work to convince a woman to sleep with them. The reason for this could be because there are still a lot of people out there who aren't promiscuous. There are also, thankfully, many who know that sex goes better with love, and that the safest sex may be abstinence. However, there are still quite a few salivating Hot Dogs out running the streets with no regard for how they may be putting themselves at physical, emotional, or spiritual risk.

Doggietales: Marcellus, age 29

Brenda was a woman I met at the bank one rainy Thursday afternoon last winter. She had long wavy hair that extended all the way down her back. She was standing in the line in front of

39

me, and all I could think about was how good her butt looked in that skirt she was wearing. There was no way I was going to let her leave that bank without trying to make her acquaintance. I made my move, and I guess she liked what I had to say because she gave me her number in record time. A week later she invited me over her house to watch videos. We were sitting there watching movies and eating popcorn like we were at the theater when one thing turned into another and then our clothes were all over the living room floor! Just then, the phone rang right in the middle of us doing our thing. I told her not to answer it, but she picked it up anyway. It was her fiance who called. We never stopped having sex, even while she was talking to him. She ended the conversation by telling the guy that she loved him and was looking forward to seeing him when he got back from Florida. She hung up the phone and we really started going at it like crazy. I didn't quite know what to make out of this whole situation, at first. So rather than trying to figure it all out, I just decided to forget about it and enjoy the moment. To this day, whenever my friends ask me how was it she was supposed to be so much in love with her fiance and still have no problems being with me, I still don't really know the answer. The only thing I can guess is that even though her "love" was out of town, her lust was still local.

Marcellus's story may seem kind of comical, but it's still rather disturbing when you really look at it. Even though Camille's behavior makes her more obviously reprehensible, Marcellus is no bargain either. The fact that he didn't have much trouble adjusting to this morally ambiguous situation makes his motivations suspect too. If you choose to pick a Hot Dog, you're going to learn the hard way how difficult it can be to give your heart to someone who may only want your body. If you hook up with these types for lovers, you're not going to get too far.

Top Dogs

Top Dogs are people who have enrolled or graduated from obedience school. They're individuals who have learned either the hard way or the easy way what it takes to be well-rounded enough to maintain a worthwhile relationship. Some of these folks weren't always at the top of the pack. Many had to go thru the school of hard knocks several times before life succeeded in knocking some sense into them. They are living proof that it is possible to find out what doing the right things in a relationship is by first doing the wrong things. Imagine that! Here's a group of people who have actually chosen to learn from their past.

Better still, there are also a number of bachelors and bachelorettes who have enough wisdom to know intrinsically how real love should look, act, and behave. Contrary to rumor, it isn't always necessary to learn things the hard way in order to further your life's education. It's possible to gain wisdom by seeing rather than suffering. That old cliche about experience that we've all heard so much isn't really true at all. Experience isn't always the best teacher, it's just the harshest.

Top Dogs are on top because they know how they want to be treated. As a result of this self-knowledge, they also have a pretty good idea about how they should treat others. Top Dogs are people that are available and single. They are the types that you would love to take home to mother. They have a healthy amount of self-control and maturity. Their maturity is the result of them having " tamed" themselves. The reward for their taking responsibility for their own behavior is their growth in character. The by-products of their character is self-respect and confidence in both who they are, and their abilities.

Interestingly, the average person with Rabid Dog symptoms usually convince themselves that the people that they meet with Top Dog qualities are too good to be true. Top Dogs are an amalgamation of all the qualities that you look for in someone worthy of spending the rest of your life with.

Doggietales: Marvin, age 32:

To be honest, I really didn't know what I was looking for at first. I kept meeting and dating a bunch of girls who were wrong for me. It seemed as if every other girl I met was still strung out over the last guy they were involved with. It was touch and go out there for awhile, but I'd go thru it all over again just to meet Wandra. When I met Wandra, everything was gravy. I had been searching for someone for years, yet when I met Wandra it didn't take me long at all to realize that she was what I was looking for all the time. The constant struggle to find someone I could get along with was starting to really get tome. It was a relief to find someone I didn't have to fight to love. A lot of women that I had been meeting are so immature that they couldn't be happy with me unless I was willing to fight with them over every minute detail concerning our relationship. See, to them, it wasn't love unless a man could stand up to them and meet all their challenges. With me, it wasn't a question of could I, but would I. I had made up my mind that I would never be with a woman who thinks that being in love is the same as being in a fight. I personally don't feel a need to be challenged every time I see my woman. If I want someone to pick a fight with me all I gotta do is brave the cruel world and go to work every day. But I expect to be respected and feel at peace when I'm with the woman in my life. Wandra gives me all that and more, which is why I'm marrying her.

Doggietales: Wandra, age 33:

Let me tell you, when Marvin blew into my life it was like a breath of fresh air. People always used to say that you have to kiss a lot of frogs before you meet a prince, but you don't have to when you can see their warts from miles away! My dad told me a long time ago to never marry a man unless he treated me how my dad treats my mom. Its kinda amazing how this thing with me and Marvin got started. My love for Marvin wasn't something that struck me all at once. True, it was lust at first sight, but I'm smart enough to know that it takes more than sexual attraction to keep me interested. From the very start, I noticed how Marvin exuded such an easy-going confidence that made me feel very relaxed and open around him. Marvin was different, very different. Marvin never tried to buy my affections never tried to use me just for a sex toy, and definitely never hit me. What Marvin did do was be there for me emotionally, cherish me, and love me so completely that its easy for me to believe that he thinks of me as an extension of himself. Marvin is the right man for me, without a doubt. I'm looking forward to marrying a man ho wants to love me so completely, because that's exactly how my dad loves mom.

Someone old and wise once said that whenever a pupil is really ready to learn in school, the instructor immediately steps into the classroom. In other words, when the time is right, everyone of us is given an opportunity to learn an important life-lesson and advance to the next level of our personal growth. in the Doggietales told previously, both Marvin and Wandra learned their lessons well. Marvin learned by trial and error, while Wandra learned by listening to wise counsel once and never doubting. They were both on two different roads that led to the same destination. Now everybody's happy. Together, they are the epitome of romantic success. They've reached the top. This is why you can call them Top Dogs!

As is evidenced by the broad range of Dogtypes listed in this chapter, dogs come in many shapes and sizes. These categories could easily be extended well into the twenties, and possibly even the thirties, rather that just leaving it just a top ten list. However, our main focus will remain on the aforementioned ten, as they are the most dominant types. It also should be clear that no person can really be entirely described as one Dogtype only. In all fairness, we as human beings are a bit too complicated to be totally pigeonholed into just one category. However, we would be in an acute state of denial if we didn't admit that we all, without exception, behave in ways that identify us more as one Dog type than another. So whichever collar fits you best, wear it!

Chapter 3
Mutt Magnets

Imagine yourself curled up in the fetal position next to the woman you've been dating the past nine months. As you lie next to her, you can hear the familiar sound of her gritting her teeth and continuously rubbing her feet together. These are the nightly, audible clues that you recognize so clearly that signal to you that she's in deep sleep. It's no secret to you that she wants to get married. As the months have gone by, she finds subtle little ways of letting you know that she wants to tie the knot sooner rather than later. Again, the same anxious thought comes racing thru your brain. You wonder what would happen if you put a ring on her finger today only to discover that she really was the wrong person to spend the rest of your life with tomorrow. How can you be sure that the woman sleeping next to you really really wants to marry you in the name of love rather than in pursuit of status? How do you know whether or not she was telling you the truth when she told you that she was no longer concerned with "keeping up with the Joneses" like she was the last time you two dated? How can you know whether or not she is the right breed of person to mate with for you?

Picture yourself and the man you're engaged to out on one of your regularly scheduled Saturday nite dates. Every time you lower your head to take another bite of chef's salad you can't help but see with your peripheral vision how he keeps flirting with the hostess who seated you earlier. In your heart, you can't help but feel those chronic pangs of insecurity and jealousy that always seem to hit you whenever you're out with him. In this most common of circumstances your mind tells you that this has happened before. In fact, your memory doesn't betray you at all, it constantly reminds you that this scenario repeats itself every time the two of you go out. The hostess is fine, true enough, but you're no slouch either. You eat right, you live right, and you're definitely no stranger to the fitness spa. You see, in your heart you know that this man has been completely remorseless about all the times you've caught him cheating on you. Every time he has apologized for his sexual indiscretions there was always a conceited smirk on his face that made you cringe on the inside. Both of you seemed to have an unspoken understanding of each other's mind set concerning your relationship. In your mind, you know that he not only doesn't know the definition of "monogamous" but he also can't even spell it! On the other hand, he knows that you are a pushover who so craves a lasting commitment from a man that you are willing to overlook anything he does as long as he eventually marries you! Almost loud enough to deafen you, you hear the words of his promise to marry you ringing in your ears as you pretend not to notice him slipping the hostess his work number. How can you be sure that he will change his ways once you marry him? Which should you allow to determine whether or not you should stay in this relationship, the things you hear him say or the things you see him do?

When two people find true love, it is a very emotional and spiritual event. Every moonlight dinner engagement, every casual touch, and every passionate kiss represents the opening of a door to a whole new chapter in the lives of the couple involved. But before you know it, the flights of fantasy that new love inspires eventually changes into a sobering song of cruel world reality when the fever of initial of infatuation fades. As the emotional turbulence of many a whirlwind love affair settles to a light breeze, then comes the time of evaluation. This is the time when everyone begins to wonder whether or not the continuance of the relationship is in their best interests. Every single person who has ever been in a long-term romance, whether they are either making or breaking a commitment, has been faced with this question. It is a sad truth that most of us insist on picking the wrong people to love and then have the nerve to blame everybody but ourselves for our choices. People customarily come to the realization that their love life may be going to the dogs when they start questioning the merit of their relationship all the time. Could the truth be that you yourself are partly responsible?

Animal Magnetism

Do you have animal magnetism? Do you attract animals? Is your real problem the fact that you both appeal to, and find appealing, people who mean you absolutely no good whatsoever? An oddball question this may seem, but the validity of which can't be argued. How else can many of our attractions and fascinations for rabid relationships be explained? Multitudes of hopeless men rush blindly into doomed love affairs with the wrong women like moths to a flame. Numerous amounts of naive women fly into the arms of the wrong men like Kamikazes on suicide missions. An uncountable number of people in our society are stricken with a malady that has damaged their perceptions. Less than perfect love-life experiences or lack of knowledge has obscured the vision of many to the point where they don't have any idea what a wholesome relationship looks like. It's true, there are lots of folks who have blind spots to bad character, in others and themselves.

Are You a Mutt Magnet?

Are you a mutt Magnet? A Mutt Magnet is a person who attracts people into their life that dog them out. Mutt Magnets are a breed of Rabid Dogs that make love choices before they've taken their Rabies shot. Mutt Magnets are folks infected by the abuses heaped upon them by other aggressive Dogtypes into thinking that the abuse and disrespect they have received is okay. In a sense, Mutt Magnets have actually been partially brainwashed that a sickly relationship is a healthy one.

Mutt Magnets isn't just a catchy phrase, it's a law. The law of Mutt Magnetism states that if a person enters into new relationships before taking the necessary steps to counteract the harmful effects of love affairs from the past, they are destined to attract people into their lives that will hurt them in the same way. It's a spiritual truth that thru a series of crises the soul grows. If life can be made analogous to a huge, multi-level skyscraper, then consider each floor as a higher level of growth and the stairs in between the lessons learned as we climb to each level of maturity. There is no skipping over stairs as we ascend to our next level of human development. God, it seems, has made it so that the doors to each floor remain locked until we have learned to use the keys we've forged from the knowledge gained from past experiences to open them. In other words, if we never learn we never grow. Sometimes, learning from the past requires more of a commitment to personal growth than many people are willing to make. Rarely is it a process done with ease. If it were really painless, it would not be such an anxiety-filled undertaking. Even a fool knows that one characteristic of an easy thing to do is that it is done more often. Many Mutt Magnets would rather continue to sleep within the "temporary" bliss of ignorance than to awaken and shoulder the 'burden" of knowledge. Mutt Magnets hide behind a wall of confusion that they have built for themselves brick by brick each time they've chosen the distraction of entering into new relationships over self examination. It's always more exciting to a Mutt Magnet to entertain someone they think they want rather than to assertain what it is they really need.

Pooper Scoopers

What is a Pooper Scooper? If you guessed a Pooper Scooper is a shovel/container type device that dog owners carry with them in the park to dispose of their pet's waste materials then you're only half-right. For our purposes, a Pooper Scooper is a professional mess cleaner! In a sick way, they secretly take a warped pride in their ability to hide the glaring faults in their romances from the peering eyes of others looking from the outside. Everybody knows at least one or two people like this. These are the people who put on the happy face and wear the fake smiles in public in order to conceal the hidden emotional pain they endlessly endure at the hands of their boyfriends or girlfriends who are dogging them out in secret. Some Pooper Scoopers are so into their charade and so full of foolish pride that they even brag about the "perfection " of their relationship to make their friends jealous. But if they only knew, it wouldn't be jealously they'd be feeling. Only pity. Pooper Scoopers put themselves in a very unenviable position. Traditionally, by the time they are willing to be honest with their friends about the truth of their relationship, the doo doo they've been shoveling and hiding has already been stinking so bad that no one can stand the smell. Rare is the friend who rushes to the aid of someone who puts on airs. Rarer still is the friend who can actually succeed in offering advice that a Pooper Scooper will heed in order to either save or escape an abusive relationship.

The Mutt Magnet Test

To determine if you are a Mutt Magnet, all that is required of you is that you take a simple test. Honestly answer the following questions. If your answer is "yes" to any of them, then it's a strong possibility you may need to be demagnetized!

1. Do you put golddigging before souldigging?
2. Do you pick a dog before you know whether or not it's the right dog for you?
3. Do you pick dogs that are already tied to something or someone else?
4. Are you more in love with your dog's prize-winning potential than their present puppy power?
5. Do you love your dog more than your dog loves you?
6. Are you a Golden Retriever?

For a better understanding of each of these test questions, let's take a more indepth look.

1. Do you put golddigging before souldigging?

For those who refuse to look in a mirror and for those who honestly can't recognize what a golddigger really looks like, let us now define the term.

A golddigger is an individual who chooses dates or mates soley for their money. Although the number of men mining for gold increases daily, statistics still show that females continue to corner the market on golddigging. It must be quickly pointed out that not all women are this money hungry, it's just that those who are so vocal about it are hard to miss. Golddiggers are very proud of being on a treasure hunt, which is why they like to announce it every chance they get. Golddiggers come across as borderline egomaniacs who live under the misconception that they're all that and the world revolves around them. Relationships they enter into are only perpetuated as long as they keep getting financial dividends from it. Golddiggers are infamous for their nonstop bragging about what they get suckers to buy them on a regular basis. The "gifts" they brag about cover a wide spectrum of monetary value. Golddiggers boasts to their friends, or anybody else who'll listen, just as loud when they receive a new necklace as when they receive a new Lexus. When these people are given the choice between love or money, they become paralyzed with uncertainty.

The segments of the female population that are well-trained in the techniques of golddigging are so skillful because they're not new at this. These particular women are brought up golddigging. As little girls, they were enthusiastically advised to either marry a doctor or a lawyer. This counseling was no doubt given to them by other golddiggers who went out of their way to teach these young girls that a man's title is more notable than his integrity. Golddiggers are frequently seen trying to outrun each other in pursuit of the man who can award them the biggest cash prize. They are very much like sprinters, in a way. Indeed, they are also similar to Olympic athletes. They always go for the gold!

Doggietales: Zena, age 38

Bruce was the most eligible bachelor in town before we were married four years ago. I was a teller working in the bank he was presiding over when I first met him. I had my sights set on him ever since that day. In fact, the main reason I took the bank job was to meet available rich men in the city and use those meetings as a way to marry me one. Bruce was a bank president in his mid-fifties whom I found out was recently divorced. I made it my business to attend every social event he attended until he took an interest in me. I'm a woman who enjoys the finer things in life, and I need a man, who can afford to keep me pampered. My momma always told me that it was just as easy to marry a rich man as it is a poor one. So I figured I would marry for money. That was four long years ago. Now, Bruce and I have two little girls that he never seems to have time for. I always thought that once we had a family he would cut down on the hours he put in at the bank to spend more time with me. I'm beginning to think the only thing he cares about is money.

Isn't it ironic? The very thing that made Zena go for Bruce turned out to be the same thing that's making her sick of him. Her first choice was money and her second choice was love. As time passed, Zena was unable to buy enough things to fill the void in her relationship created by Bruce's lack of emotional involvement. The lesson learned is that money can't blind you to the imperfections of your relationship forever. It can only make them harder to see. What is most important to you, love or money? You have to either be on one side or the other. There is no fence to ride when it comes to making decisions on matters of the heart.

2. Do you pick a dog before you know whether or not it's the right dog for you?

The road to many unfulfilling relationships and broken marriages is littered with the remains of hapless people who've made premature commitments. Do you have a habit of moving too fast? Have you ever been guilty of jumping the gun? People who plead guilty to this offense are traditionally those who have only a partial idea of what they're seeking in a partner. The wisest option any person can ever choose is to actually make a conscious effort to figure out what specific combination of attributes in another person will satisfy their relationship requirements. The operative word in the previous sentence is "attributes" with an "s". There is no true connection that exists between two people that can be sustained solely on the presence of one quality. It takes an amalgamation of spiritual, mental, physical, and emotional traits, existing in each partner to give any relationship a fighting chance for survival. People who don't have a clearly drawn mental picture of what they really want in a lover often can't control their excitement when they're able to perceive one quality in someone they've been looking for. Gazing into the direction of their current lover, these individuals see one characteristic and then declare that their search is over. Their rush to judgment causes them to put commitment before compatibility.

Infatuation is a superficial attraction for another person that's based only on an irrational passion. Infatuation, many times, occurs as a preliminary event possibly heralding the arrival of true love. The key word to consider here is " possibly". Since infatuation is such a shallow stage in romantic development, it should be not surprising that it comes with no guarantee for true love. You know you've made relationship choices based on infatuation when you find yourself making statements like these:

"The way Rolanda moved on the dance floor was like no one I'd ever met before! The sultry, sexy way she swerved her hips reminded me of all those girls I love to watch in music videos."

"The first time I saw Jeremy I was stunned by just how gorgeous he looked in the suit he was wearing. I don't know what it is , but I'm a sucker for a man in a nice suit."

The clothes a person wears, the way someone's voice sounds, how much rhythm somebody has, the haircut someone has-- are any of these superficial qualities substantial enough to sustain a real relationship? Of course not. However, a bunch of folks let infatuation with something about a person cause them to ignore who that person really is inside. After all, how long can someone keep wearing the same suits and doing the same dances before it starts to get old? After awhile, you'll want to see what's below the surface. And if they have nothing else in common with you, it'll be a disappointing discovery.

Interestingly, men seem to bear the heavier burden of the "If one thing is good, then it's all good" mentality. Women at least, even shallow women, eventually reach a point in their lives when they realize that a certain balance of qualities is vital to maintaining a lasting relationship. Men, however, seem to be a lot slower on the uptake. There are some men who can go for decades completely satisfied with a woman of no intellectual capacity as long as she has unlimited sexuality. For the men for whom this statement is true, change is not an easy process.

Just like there are some women who are golddiggers, there are also some men who are bootybuyers. Bootybuyers are people, usually men, who are willing to pay any price necessary to gain ownership to whatever attribute they desire most in a partner. The quality desired can cover a wide range such as a nice body, a college education, a classy demeanor, a pretty face, etc. Bootybuyers aren't really concerned about other characteristics in a person because they feel that once they pay for one item, the others are usually thought of as nonessentials. Other qualities are thought of as accessories at best. To them, it"s all a package deal.

Doggietales: Devon, age 39

I thought I had finally done it. I thought I had succeeded in pulling the perfect lady into my life. Cheri was a girl so fine that every time I saw her she gave me a gasface. (A gasface is the look you get on your face when you see a lady with measurements so impressive that it hurts you to see her! I mean, it actually pains you in your gut not to have her!) The first day I met her I decided to go on a mission to make her mine. I found out Cheri worked as a stripper and she was used to guys approaching her all the time. It took me almost eight months just to get her to agree to a date. I spent more time and money chasing Cheri than I'm willing to admit to anybody who knows me. It was like an obsession. Her body was incredible. When the night came the we finally had sex, I was happier than a kid at Disney World! Well, we made love and it turned out to be the most frustrating thing I've ever experienced. You see, Cheri, the stripper who oozed pure sexuality, wasn't sexy in bed at all. To Cheri, sex was her job, and although she would sleep with me out of a feeling of "girlfriend" obligation, she didn't enjoy it all. Sex with Cheri was boring and lackluster. It's no thrill at all being with someone who's making you feel like she's doing you a favor by sleeping with you. I swear, if she hadn't have gotten pregnant I probably would have left her by now.

Devon bought the wrong booty, it seems. Unfortunately, people don't come with ingredient labels or sales receipts. Some items bootybuyers purchase can't be returned. Sometimes when you buy something outright, it and all the accessories that come with it are yours from now on. Always invest the time it takes to really get to know the whole person, not just parts of them.

Remember Laissez-Faire. Let The Buyer Beware, because it's a package deal!

    3.   Do you pick dogs that are already tied to something or someone else?

Do you go out and purposely find someone you know who could never be yours? Do you pick people you know you can't have? Many do this because they themselves are Rabid Dogs and don't want to be hurt again. When someone is afraid of love, nothing is safer than picking somebody with whom they know they can have no future. This seems to be a ridiculous premise on the surface, but it's really amazing what actually motivates people's behavior on a subconscious level.

Choosing lovers who aren't really free to be chosen is the same as applying for a job that's already taken. It is also the equivalent of seeking a promotion at a job you already know has a glass ceiling. Somewhere in the back of your mind you already know there's no room for advancement. Some prospects are married, some are living with someone, some are proud workaholics, and some claim they are just coming out of a relationship. By the way, since it's just been mentioned, never date someone who says they are just coming out of a relationship. Either they're still involved or they're not. This "coming out" stuff is usually a smoke screen used to hide the fact they may be heading back! Be especially wary when dealing with these people, because if they really were out of the relationship they will have closed the door behind them. Whenever people consciously or subconsciously go out of their way to find partners who can't really be with them exclusively, they're really asking to get their feelings hurt.

Why do men and women select individuals they can't have? There are really only two major reasons for this phenomenon.

A. You're scared to get too close

A large number of people have suffered so much pain in previous romantic commitments that they have decided that they will never put themselves in a position where they'll ever be hurt again. As a result people who are afraid to get too close make a habit of picking lovers whom they can never truly be intimate with. This is an undercover way of shielding themselves from the possible pain of a bad relationship.

B. You don't think much of yourself

There is a scripture in the Bible that says," As a man thinks, so is he." This, of course, is also true of women. The relationships men and women choose act as mirrors reflecting what they honestly think of themselves. If the reflection staring back reveals a person with low self-esteem, then it's a strong possibility that the only reason they're even in this relationship is because they may feel it's all they deserve.

The bottom line is that when you pick dogs that are already tied to something or someone else, the most you'll ever be able to get is leftover table scraps from someone else's main dish.

4. Are you more in love with your dog's prize winning potential than their present puppy power?

"People think Cynthia can be a real bitch sometimes, but that's only because it takes a special kind of person to really understand where she's coming from. These people just don't know, Cynthia can be a very friendly person if you just take the time to get to know her. I mean, on her good days, it's really easy for everybody else to see why I love her so much!"

"I've always known Dewayne really loves me, even though he never says it. It's just that he's a real macho guy and he's just not into wearing his feelings on his sleeve. I just believe that if I stick with him for a while longer he'll finally feel free enough to open his heart to me and tell me he loves me. It's only a matter of time."

"Sherrecia is the type of lady I have always wanted. Years of working as a photographer has given me a real thing for models. Sherrecia is a lovely lady in every way. It took me months to convince her to pose for me and send her pictures to the magazine for submission. As soon as I get the reply back I'm sure she'll get over her natural shyness and model lingerie full time. After all, why wouldn't she want to be admired all the time for her exotic beauty? When she signs that lucrative modeling contract she'll be the perfect image of what I want in a woman!"

If any of these exercises in wishful thinking seem too familiar then it may be because you've been doing them yourself. You probably are one of those individuals well-acquainted with the experience of falling in love with somebody's potential. People who get caught in this trap aren't really in love with who their lover is today, but rather who they may become tomorrow. For years, some people have made it a favorite pastime to go out and find people to love that they consider "works in progress." When these "people under development" are found, the individuals who sought them out then proceed to do whatever it takes to develop them. They fool themselves into believing that they're doing the other person a favor. It's clear to them that these lovers are in need of help that only they can provide. The entire purpose of these kinds of relationships is to create an atmosphere in which one person can choose to consciously and comfortably ignore the truth about who the other person really is.

Contract Jobs

Actually, these associations aren't really relationships at all, they're contract jobs. A contract job is a form of employment, usually temporary, that applicants choose to accept until the job is done. Once the contract is up , the job is done, and it's on to the next one. Many people who prefer these kinds of couplings are, in a sense, workaholics. They won't be satisfied until the work is done. However, once the improvement job is finished, so is the relationship.

It's an extremely addictive situation that these types of relationships produce. Like a drug addict, some people get sprung on the rush that comes from not knowing when all the work you've done to help someone else reach their potential will suddenly pay off. Like someone who bets on horse races or someone who plays the lottery, you constantly tell yourself your big payday is always just around the corner. It's an actual obsession.

There are three main reasons why certain Mutt Magnets tend to gravitate toward these kinds of relationships:

You have the "I can't win" syndrome.

Somewhere along the line as you have lived your romantic life, you've had so many repeated unfulfilling relationships that you are now falsely convinced that you can never pick a winner. As a result, you instinctly choose people who either can't fulfill your relationship wishes, or elect not to try. The vicious circle that encompasses you is one that has you continually trying to improve people you always feel need improvement. You can never be satisfied with that person because, to you, they're forever "a work in progress". The only conceivable way you'll be with yesterday's lover today is if you think they can some way be new and improved.

You have the "I manipulate" syndrome.

The overused term "control freak" is applicable here. When you enter into relationships with the attitude that you are on a higher level than the other person, you have a sense of supremacy. People who think they are so much better than their lovers are seeking to "better" them because they get off on the feeling of power and control it gives them. Even if on the surface it doesn't seem this way, just the idea that your partner doesn't have it going on enough for you the way they are now puts you in the manipulator's position. Most manipulators think they have absolute power, and absolute power corrupts the purity of a romance absolutely.

You have the " forget about me" syndrome.

There's no better way to distance yourself from your own faults and imperfections than to overly concern yourself with working on those of others. Rather than concentrating on fixing and improving your own life, it's always more entertaining to screw around with someone else's life. People like these make a habit of constantly rationalizing away the reasons why they haven't achieved their personal goals by insisting that their time and attention is more well-spent improving someone else's life. These folks find it strangely more rewarding to "help" someone else achieve their goals by neglecting their own. Remember, procrastination is a luxury that personally ambitious men and women can't afford.

Doggietales: Paul, age 32

I met April the very next fall that followed the end of Desert Storm. It was nice to be back home in the states and away from those deadly situations. April was in law school and was very excited about one day practicing law, preferably for some big corporation. I was attending the same university studying pre-med. In Desert Storm I had more than a few incidents occur where I had to medically attend to some of my comrades. In fact, I was even blessed to be able to help save a close friend's life once while over there. That's what gave me the urge to study medicine and possibly become a doctor. Over the next year and a half, April and I dated exclusively. We even talked marriage on more than one occasion. That's when something happened that changed my life. On the way home from one of our dates, I came upon a intersection where a car wreck happened right in front of me. I guess it was instinct, because rather than run and call for an ambulance, I ran onto the scene and started doing what I could to help the people involved. Someone else must have called for the ambulance because they managed to arrive on the scene within ten minutes. By the way though, I had already bandaged one guy and had thankfully been able to revive the lady who was riding in the car with him thru CPR. The paramedics came and took over, but later complemented me on my skills and quick-thinking. After that day, I decided I'd rather be a paramedic than a doctor. It was something about being able to help people on the spot, the immediacy of it all, that really appealed to me. When I told April I had decided not to be a doctor there was no way she could hide her disappointment. Over the course of the next few months she let it be known that she thought I was throwing my future away and could do much more with my life than be "just a paramedic". Well, it should come as no surprise that our relationship didn't last much longer after that. I'm a paramedic now and I know I made the right choice with my career. Me, my friends, and my family are all very proud of the man I have become. It's too bad the only

60

person who's disappointed in who I am today is the woman I once wanted to marry.

Being in a great romantic relationship is a result of loving who people are now, not who you hope they'll be tomorrow.

5.   Do you love your dog more than your dog loves you?

There is such a thing as emotional equilibrium in every relationship.   People never offer anyone anything of worth without the expectation of receiving something of equal worth in return.   This is not a self-indulgence, but another form of self-respect.   In all fairness, it must be pointed out that something of worth received in reciprocation of a loving act can wear many disguises.   Adequate compensation can be anything from giving money, to giving a massage.   For example, people who bravely risked their own lives to rush to the aid of recent flood victims did so because it made them feel worthy and valuable as fellow human beings, not because they were getting paid to do it.   There are some situations wherein people will sacrifice and give themselves in ways they never would if money were the only incentive.

The Art of Throwing and Fetching Equally

There's no way around it, the truth of the matter is that we show love to someone hoping that we'll be shown love back. The throwing and fetching of love between two people doesn't have to always be perfectly even.   What is important is whether or not participants are getting enough of what they need from each other to make them happy.   However, when one individual gives too much to someone who gives too little, it will only be a matter of time before feelings of contempt and inferiority erode the relationship.   The person who receives an overabundance of love that they know they've done very little to deserve feels contempt for the one who's giving it.   On the other hand, the person who is constantly compelled to shower someone with love who shows no real appreciation for it can't help but feel inferior or unworthy to the object of their affections. Relationships can only progress as long as each person continues to shoulder the amount of weight necessary to maintain proper balance. Anything less than this puts an undue amount of stress and strain on one of the lovers. This what is meant by being unequally yoked.

Welcome To Romance Theater

It is said that all the world is just a stage and we are merely players. Are you an actor or an audience member? If you said you are an actor, you're in a very unenviable position. If you said you are an audience member, congratulations, you are in an even worse position. Welcome to romance theater, where everyone is either an actor or audience member interchangeably throughout the courtship. The actor is the one who takes it upon themself to both perform to the satisfaction of and cater to the needs of the other person. The actor is the one responsible for putting on the show and pleasing the other person. They often sacrifice their wants and needs in deference to those of the other lover. The audience member is the one who is sitting on the throne waiting to be pleased and catered to. If you take a mental survey of the people in relationships you know, it's a fairly simple process to figure out which ones in the couple that are in the role of actor or audience member. It is a sexually ambiguous role. Male or female can fit easily into either character part. Neither is one individual constantly in one role or the other, although one role more than the other usually is chosen more consistently by one person in every couple. Sometimes it is also circumstantial, and more often than not interchangeable. It is not unusual to see actors become audience members and audience members become actors. Being Top Dog in any relationship is a matter of making sure you spend as much time sitting in the audience as you do performing on stage.

A variety of circumstances often occur that help to create a potentially unfulfilling romantic relationship. When two audience members meet each other in the front row of romance theater and neither one assumes the role of actor, then the most they can hope for is to see a short play. Really, it can only be a play with a very exciting first act that once it reaches intermission, the two people involved never take to the stage because they're waiting for the other to act! When love isn't acted upon, it eventually dies. These are typically the whirlwind romances that start off with gusts so strong that they blow themselves out. Actor/audience member relationships that are more lopsided in favor of one lover than the other are also destined for disaster due to the fact that they are so lopsided.

When two actors meet each other on stage in romance theaters is when love is at it's most gratifying and invigorating. What follows is an exercise of perfectly balanced giving and taking that is both fascinating to watch and energizing to experience. This kind of love is not for cowards. It takes a courageous amount of personal, emotional, and spiritual growth to willingly risk loving this unselfishly. People who claim they really want lasting love always begin their love affairs this way on one level, but customarily on another level ultimately start sabotaging everything they've worked for. These folks make the fatal mistake of letting boredom, mistrust, and carelessness choke the life out of their romance. Every relatively mature person knows to some extent what it takes to maintain a good relationship, but rare is the man or woman bold enough to do it.

If you are more in love with someone than they are with you, then you're no stranger to the fear of abandonment. Only someone afraid to be by themselves would fight so hard to stay in a lopsided relationship where they settle for less than what they want so quickly and quietly. Every relationship has times when one person is more into it than the other. If it's a healthy romance, those times come and go with a subtle frequency as each person takes turns giving and taking. But, it's nothing but a bad situation when one individual constantly overextends him or herself just to get a few crumbs of love in return.

Doggietales: Samantha, age 36:
I did my best, it just wasn't good enough. I loved Eric from the first date we went out on. He was the person I wanted to spend the rest of my life with. Eric was everything to me. So

63

what if he never seemed to be as excited about our relationship as I was, I thought that I had enough love in me for both of us. When we finally married, I made it my business to support him in everything he did. I let him know that his happiness was the most important   thing to me.   Whenever he took jobs that required us to move out of town, I supported him. When he made fun of me and embarrassed me in front of our friends, I didn't complain. Even when I found out he was cheating on me with my best friend, I kept it to myself and never uttered a word against what he was doing. So when the day came he filed for divorce, I was devastated. How could he be so cruel to someone who loved him as much as I did?

Samantha's failed marriage is almost as painful to hear about as it probably was for her to live thru. Samantha learned in the most excruciatingly painful way that you aren't guaranteed that people will love you just because you love them. They have to also be convinced that you are a whole person that is worth their love. Are you a whole person? Respect precedes love, and since Samantha was apparently not respected much at all, Eric never loved her. The only thing Eric seemed to have for Samantha was contempt. Samantha allowed herself to be increasingly devalued until she became a non-person in Eric's eyes. She made a habit of emotionally undressing in front of someone who didn't really care about her. She chose to remain silent when confronted with outrageous acts of disrespect. She was also choosing to endure quiet desperation for fear of losing him. Everyone involved would have been better served if she had spoken up. They say that silence is golden, but sometimes it's just yellow.

6. Are You a Golden Retriever?

Imagine yourself sitting onboard a crowded airplane. As you travel coast to coast, you pull out your state-of-the-art walkman cassette player with headphones. When you're sure no one is looking, you quickly slip a top-secret cassette into your tape player. You set the volume at a level that insures you that no ears but yours can hear the voice filling your headphones.

The message on the tape says, " Your mission, if you choose to accept it, is to actively seek a person to have a relationship with that's in need of help that only you can give them. The person you choose can have any type of problem you prefer. It can be emotional, mental, spiritual, financial, or whatever. The most vital part of choosing the right person to fall in love with for this mission is that you feel sorry for them. Your reward for saving the person out of their dilemma is that they will be eternally grateful to you for the rest of their lives. For security purposes, this tape will self-destruct in fifteen seconds."

If you thought this sounds an awful lot like a scene from an old Mission Impossible episode you're right in more ways than one. Indeed, no mission is more impossible to accomplish than to retrieve love by going on a rescue mission. Does any of this sounds familiar? Do you find yourself always going on rescue missions? Golden retrievers are people who look at every potential romance as bright, shiny, and golden despite any glaring evidence to the contrary. Golden Retrievers are always gung ho about hooking up with someone they feel an obligation to save, as opposed to someone who can stand on their own. They love to seek out people who are hurt, vulnerable, or emotionally abandoned. Golden Retrievers are Mutt-Magnets who are attracted to the idea of loving the presently unlovable. Golden Retrievers are somewhat similar to people who love people for their potential rather than who they are now. The difference lies in the fact that Golden Retrievers are much more focused and specific about the things in their lovers that need to be fixed. Also, Golden Retrievers actually feel a kind of "love" for the person they're rescuing simply because they need rescuing.

As has been clearly shown, rescue missions are not just the stuff of which action/adventure films are made of, but real-life relationships as well. Real-life rescue missions, just like those on film, often result in dire consequences. The outcome of a botched rescue mission is the sense of betrayal that is felt by the person who does the rescuing. Golden Retrievers often end up feeling like stepping stones. They feel used because they are customarily discarded after their usefulness is at an end. The truth is that they chose to set themselves up for such a fall by putting themselves in such a vulnerable position. However, successful rescue missions have a negative fallout as well. There is always a downside. There is always a love casualty. The person who makes the successful rescue feels an overwhelming sense of let down once they have succeeded. Ultimately, they begin to miss the challenge and the rush they got when they first embarked on the mission. The restlessness they feel surfaces as they begin to constantly remind the other person that they will always have them to thank for rescuing them. This type of nagging conceit succeeds only in driving the person out of their lives in order to clean the slate for another rescue mission.

The Rabies Shot

The Rabies Shot is the self-indulged cure for whatever ails a person suffering from the after effects of a bad relationship. Rabies represents the infectious influence that one person leaves on another when a relationship ends. These infections that bad relationships give people can be recognized by the symptoms of an overall bad attitude, hurt feelings, and an unhealthy paranoia toward dealing with someone new. What's needed in situations like this is time to heal. A Rabies Shot is a dose of reality. The time it takes to recover from an unfulfilling relationship differs from person to person. Taking a Rabies Shot is a three-part process. The first step is to decide to no longer hide from the reality of what happened in the last failed relationship. Take an honest look at the things that were done wrong by both parties. Learn what you can from it and determine what, if anything, you can do differently next time to prevent a similar outcome. The second step is to actually grow from the experience and move on. The third and final step is to get in the new habit of changing your previously negative behavior to positive with uncompromising consistency. Anything done often enough at some point becomes second nature to the person doing it. If you change the ways you act first, the ways you feel will soon change also.

Mutt Magnetism is not a condition that is incurable. Mutt Magnets can have their polarity reversed by taking the Rabies shot. This is the only way Mutt Magnets can be reconciled to their past and be receptive to the possibilities that await them in their future.

Chapter 4
How to Know When You Are Gettin' Dogged Out!

For as long as you can remember, everyone's always told you that love is all you need. Love is the vehicle thru which all your peace, happiness, pleasure, and warmth will come. But what do you do when you're in love and it brings you nothing but pain? The "love" enthusiasts are always quick to tell you what a wonderful thing love is, but they almost never tell you the trouble that unrequited love can bring.

A major part of the joy that comes from loving someone is being loved in return. Certain things in life are given. You unselfishly love your family, and they unselfishly love you in return. You even love your pet unconditionally and your pet loves you the same way in return. However, romantic love is a different situation altogether. In loving another individual there is absolutely no unspoken agreement that they will love you back.

Few things in life that we encounter are more painful than loving someone who doesn't love you back. Nothing seems as frustrating and humiliating as knowing that the object of your affections thinks almost nothing of you at all. To be treated with indifference is the most insensitive thing that can be done to someone who is in love. Being in a one-sided love affair is a no-win situation. Perhaps the hardest thing to deal with is simply facing up to the fact that you may be getting dogged out in your relationship.

Ask yourself the following questions:

Who decides what movies you see all the time? Who chooses the group of people you always find yourself socializing with? Who's decision is it when it's time to have kids? Who decides when it's time to have sex and how often? Who rules over the money? Who's wishes are always catered to in the relationship?

69

If your response to all these inquiries is "you do," then be afraid. On the other hand, if your response to all these inquiries is "they do," then be very afraid! Remember, it's rarely ever a good thing for anyone to be living under a love dictatorship. The appropriate balance of rule should be that of a king and his queen. The best relationships are not categorized by outfighting each other, but outloving each other. But to make love and not war takes a serious commitment by each party. When one person's committed and the other isn't, usually the one who's committed is setting themselves up to be dogged out. Are you the one getting dogged out?

For those who like to pretend they don't know, there are six unmistakable ways to know when you are getting dogged out. You know you're getting dogged out when you are able to recognize signs that show that you are losing, or have totally lost your half of the power in the relationship. The shifts in the balance of power in relationships are very gradual, and therefore difficult to detect. You have to consistently make a concerted effort to be watchful. If you blink, you'll miss it. Encroachments on the sanctity of relationships can be likened to the invasion of foreigners on a sovereign nation. Just like a country, a relationship has borders. If these borders are crossed with impunity and no retribution is made, then that country is teaching the other that they are open to further affronts. To avoid such turns of events, all crimes of disrespect must be punished swiftly and severely in both national matters and matters of the heart. Any seemingly unrelated occasion of disrespect may indeed appear of minor importance to the health of the relationship at first, but over time a heavy toll is taken. Remember, it's not the single drop of rain that sweeps away your home and everything else you've worked for, it's the accumulation of raindrops that cause the flood that does it.

Vigilance is the key to safeguarding against being dogged out in any relationship. Lines of respect must be drawn clearly and protected bravely if proper balance is to be maintained. Keep your eyes open and constantly be on the lookout for these telltale signs that signal less than desirable changes in your relationship.

1.   They Don't Have Time For You Anymore

Most romantic encounters follow a specific pattern. Usually a hunter/prey type scenario is played out over a course of time. Every budding romance casts the two people involved into the roles of pursuer and pursued one. Typically, the one doing the pursuing is obviously the one who's most interested. They hunt the person they want in such a state of reckless abandon that time

71

spent in the pursuit holds no meaning. Once they've won the affections of the person they've been chasing their usual response is to bring a sudden end to the relentlessness of the hunt. Sometimes it's boredom, but most of the time the person who stops doing all those caring and romantic things they used to do in the beginning do so because they are simply so emotionally drained of energy that they need time to recuperate. It should be common knowledge that no one can continue to burn gas without ultimately taking the time necessary to refill their tank. Because they've been expending so much energy to win the object of their affection that as soon as this is done they feel a need to do other things that supply them with energy instead. These energizing activities generally include things like enjoying their lifelong hobbies and kicking it with their friends. You know, things they really, really like to do. This is a normal reaction for the person who has been doing most of the pursuing to have. After the initial firestorm that new love starts with quiets down to a steady blaze is when the two people involved can start to decide how much they're willing to do to keep it burning.

Changes in the time that a couple spend together is the most accurate barometer to use when trying to determine the health of the relationship. A person's interests as a separate person will eventually cause somewhat of a change in the amount of time a couple spends together . This is both normal and expected. However, it is the shockingly abrupt changes in time spent together that signal a real problem. It's a pretty good indication that if a person who used to be readily available to you suddenly becomes unavailable, then there's definitely something going on that they're not telling you. The answer could be anything as disappointing as they're bored with you, or something as devastating as they're cheating on you. If you're a novice gambler, you'd be well-advised to bet on the latter. The best thing to do in cases like this is to keep your eyes open for clues that something is amiss.

The wisest thing a man or woman can do in a relationship is to personally take charge of the time spent together. Either you decide the frequency of your togetherness or it will definitely be decided for you. It's your responsibility to get the attention you need to make you happy. When you're dissatisfied with the amount of time you spend together it's up to you to speak up. It's also in your best interest to take note of where you rank on your lover's priority list of important things to do. If you don't like the position you occupy on the list, then it's up to you to take swift and decisive action to fix things the way you want them. Do this early in the relationship because once being put on a back burner becomes a habit, it's harder to break.

Unfortunately, there are times in the majority of romances that it is necessary to do something shocking to wake the other person up so they won't start sleeping on the relationship. Anything that doesn't cause any real harm to the other person while at the same time puts you in the spotlight, is acceptable. Nothing snatches a person out of their comfort zone like a perceived threat to a relationship they've been taking for granted.

Doggietales: Donnel, age 23

I've been crazy about Lauren since the first day I saw her cheering for the other team at our college homecoming game. Lauren was a pom pom girl for our fiercest rival's school. I made it my business to try to hook up with her every time I saw her. I found myself going to every home game her school had. We finally started dating about four months after I started asking her out. I guess it took us so long to connect because Lauren had more than her share of brothers trying to get with her. Things were rolling smooth for us for close to a year before I started to check out how Lauren started dissin' me to do other things. At first, it hurt my feelings so bad that she was kickin' me to the curb to hang out with her friends that I didn't tell anybody what was happening. Then, one day, my older sister came to town to spend Christmas with us and I decided to talk to her about what was going on with me and Lauren. It was a very informative conversation we had as I drove my sister home from the airport. She gave me a lot of good advice and insight into the female mind that I was hoping to use in my particular situation. But, before I could get a chance to actually use it, something interesting happened with Lauren later on that day at the carwash. See, I asked Lauren to come with me to wash my car.

As was the case with her those days, she nonchalantly agreed. I was spraying the outside as she was cleaning out the inside when she found a tube of lipstick that was a color she never used. Lauren, who had previously been very indifferent towards me, suddenly got mad and confronted me about who's lipstick it was. After hours of telling her I didn't know who's it was, we finally stopped arguing and she seemed to calm down. After that, for some reason, Lauren stuck to me like she used to. That was almost a year ago, and she hasn't started taking me for granted again yet. We've never been happier. All this good stuff happened because she thought she might be losing me. But the funniest thing of all is that I found out that the mysterious tube of lipstick belonged to my sister! I guess it must have fell out of her purse when I was driving her home from the airport!

2.   Anything You Do Wrong is Unforgivable

If you think long enough, you are sure to be able to remember a time in your relationship when you could no wrong. When love is new, there is a natural tendency for two people to overlook each other's annoying habits and idiosyncrasies. If he were late for a special dinner date with you, all he had to do was crack a joke or make an amusing comment and he was automatically forgiven. If she spent all day at the mall shopping when she was supposed to be at a picnic with you, all she had to do was explain to you the reasons why only earth tone clothing matches her complexion for you to forgive her right away. Yes, that was then, but this is now. The novelty of the relationship is a thing of the past. It's true that persons who are more prone to have these sort of negative reactions to the person they're with are those with the most unrealistic views of what a relationship should be. At some point in every relationship, the novelty wears off and the things you once thought were extraordinary become commonplace.

In order to stave off familiarity breeding contempt, a sense of humor and a thirst for knowledge are your most useful tools. A sense of humor is what you need to keep your attitude adjusted properly in order to handle the subtle changes that occur in every romantic coupling. The ability to find something amusing in every potentially threatening relationship problem is useful to a certain extent, but an ever growing thirst for knowledge is more useful still. Being wise leaves a much longer lasting impression than just being witty. Knowledge can be regenerated and increased over time as we grow and mature as individuals.

There are several things that can occur that will deflate the appreciation one person has for another during the passage of time. The first is that one person be advancing in personal development quicker than the other due to employment opportunities, furthering their educations, or constantly expanding outside interests. This has the potential of being very dangerous to a couple unless the other person is going on self-improvement missions of their own. The second thing that can lower a person's opinion of their partner is when they feel their partner is satisfied with their life, while they themselves are still hungry. Once this happens, the person who's still hungry for growth will at some point start harshly criticizing the other person either out of their comfort zone, or out of the relationship. So now a situation presents itself where not only is anything the person does wrong become unforgivable, but just the fact they aren't perfect becomes a bone of contention.

In any case, know that maintenance in a relationship is always better than repair. It's also a whole lot easier. If you were "The Bomb" when your lover first met you, it's in your best interest to keep "blowing up" as much as possible. Remember, it's a cruel fact of life that if a person thinks you've got it going on, then they like you and you can do no wrong. But if they decide at some point that they don't like you, then you can do no right.

3. You Break Up To Make Up More Often

Early in the relationship, the length of time it takes to make up, even after a big argument, is negligible. Hormones are running the show while levelheadedness has been hog tied and left for dead on the side of the road somewhere. No matter how potentially damaging the disagreement, no matter how abundant the amount of arguing, nothing matters more to a new couple in love than experiencing the excitedly chemical reactions that they give each other. Little else about the relationship has more meaning. Over time, the influence of overactive hormones usually lessens to a point where the initial infatuation both people feel gives way to actual recognition of who the other person really is. Normal circumstances and everyday problems interrupt the flow of fantasy and force people to take a good long look at what they really have together.

Differences begin to matter more. Abrasive arguments tend to leave more lasting scars. Stuff about the other person that rubs you the wrong way no longer seems rare or unusual, but easily recognizable and commonplace. As a result, it becomes now more difficult to accept the other person's differences and tolerate their faults. The things about the other that used to bring a smile now brings a frown. The frequency of the good times decreases and the fights increase. Fights don't always reach the point where people come to blows, but unfortunately, sometimes this does happen. What's guarranteed to happen though, is that the underlying feelings of discontent that each person has for the other starts to block the forces of attraction that initially brought them to each other.

Sadly, the world in which we live is not an ideal one. Any couple who are a couple long enough will find some things about each other that are less than likable. However, there are some differences that can be lived with and some that can't. The trick is knowing which is which. The greater the maturity of the individual, the clearer it is to recognize the difference between true incompatibility and a chance to achieve a deeper kind of closeness. When staring into the face of true intimacy, many are struck with the impulse to fight or flee. How badly a person wants the relationship to work will determine which choice is made.

These circumstances cause the faint of heart to look for greener pastures. New love affairs are worry free. Seeing the other person is always play time. No one relishes the idea of working all day at the office only to get off and put in hours of hard labor on their love life. People who make a habit of discarding old relationships for new ones fail to realize that all relationships age, and being able to compromise and deal with differences is a skill that no one can afford not to develop.

There are a number of people who break up to make up out of an overblown love for drama. These drama lovers are individuals who confuse soap operas with real life. They have subconsciously memorized every motivation and gesture ever enacted before them by their favorite TV and movie stars. They do the finger pointing, they cry the fake tears, and they love to make the false accusations that create the distance they know they need to eventually break up with someone for good. For these, turmoil is a turn on. For them, a consistent relationship is so boring that it takes frequent breakups just to keep it interesting. Like second-string actors in a trashy TV movie, these types recite the same tired lines to get them out of every relationship. Lines like "It's not you, it's me" or "I need some time alone" are often used by professional breakup artists. The time they say they need to be alone is really just time they need away from you. Yeah, they'll tell you they're alone, but you can bet they're not lonely! Breakup artists just want you out of the way in order to make room for someone else. They are deceitful and gutless, and will never tell you the whole truth. They are confused people who really don't know what they want. When one lover breaks up and makes up with the other on a routine basis, know that they are only practicing their lines before they break up for good.

4. Sex is a Memory

Sex steering a relationship is like a tail wagging the dog. Still, it can be argued that what happens in the bedroom is a reflection of what's happening in the rest of the relationship. When two people first meet and the attraction is strong, the frequency of sex between the two is usually off the scale. It's not uncommon for two people in lust to tear each other's clothes off every time they see each other. Sex is the drug that cures whatever ails them. It's truly a blessing to find someone who has a sex drive equal to your own, but ordinarily, the passage of time helps in the determination of what a couple's shared sexual frequency will be.

It is in your best interest to do whatever you can to determine what your mate's sexual appetite is as early in the relationship as possible. However, this can be tricky, because information compiled too near the beginning of the relationship is subject to be inconclusive. When the number of sexual escapades begin to normalize, only then will a noticeable frequency rate emerge.

Which one of you gets the notion to get your groove on first will at this point become a factor too important to be ignored. Once sex has begun, how interested is the other person in what's going on? How imaginative and how resourceful is the other person in making it a mutually enjoyable experience? If it is always the same, and boringly mechanical, then underlying trouble may be brewing.

What's Good About Marital Sex

Marriage, a totally committed relationship between two people under God forsaking all others, is the first institution ever created. It is said that only in this instance can two become one. To folks who haven't desensitized themselves by abusing it, sex is an extremely bonding experience. The unifying qualities of good sex cover a wide spectrum of positive attributes. Sex brings two people together mentally, emotionally, spiritually, and physically. Sexuality treated callously and casually is not a good thing. But when it is enjoyed within the confines of a committed, monogamous relationship, studies show that it can be a great thing.

What's Dangerous About Premarital Sex

    Noncommittal sex is like playing roulette, the Russian kind. You never really know when you'll spin the barrel and blow your brains out. Sure, the relationship may be going smoothly now and the sex may be great, but what will keep the other person there when the hard times that every relationship goes thru occurs. Lack of a lasting commitment provides the least determined partner the perfect escape hatch thru which they can

79

bail out of a potentially fulfilling relationship. It doesn't take a genius to figure out that all people run because they are afraid. Making a real vow of marriage is something that the average sex enthusiast is fearful of because they know that their selfishness will have to take a back seat to compromise. It's easy to "love" someone while you're having sex with them, but no one can stay in bed 24 hours a day. As time passes, lack of commitment breeds chronic distrust. As a result, sex metamorphosizes into a meal ticket, a bargaining chip, a battering ram, and even an extortion attempt. In other words, sex becomes everything but a bonding experience.

When a person who used to like sex all the time begins to lose interest in it, it can be a huge blow to the ego. Could it be that they are having sex with someone else? Or, could it be that your lovemaking skills leave a bit to be desired? If a person really loves you and has enough patience, sexual technique is something that can be taught. If love making skills isn't an issue, and sex with your partner is still just a memory, then the answer could be that you are "The Bomb" when it comes to sex. Maybe your sex is so good that it takes your lover a long time to recover after you satisfy them so completely. That's a great ego trip to go on, but only in rare cases is this the cause of a reduction in sex drive. Most of the time it's because they're cheating on you or are dissatisfied with your sexual performance. If you have sex with someone and they seem unsatisfied, the only thing you can do is ask them how you can make it better. If they refuse to tell you because they feel you should know instinctively how to please them, then here's the perfect solution: Wave them goodbye. You don't need that kind of stress. If they're too uptight to open up to you, then they're much too emotionally constipated and unavailable to be a viable candidate for a healthy relationship. To willingly stay in a situation where someone keeps you jumping thru sexual hoops just to keep them interested is like asking them to dog you out.

5.   You Start Getting Taken For a Joke

A good way to know when you're gettin' dogged out is to take notice of what the other person thinks of you. What do they really think of you as an individual? Do they respect who you are? Is your opinion taken seriously or are you taken as a joke? Do people always have to remind you that you are a voice in this world and you should stand up and be heard? Does what you have to say matter or is it of no consequence to your partner. These, and many questions like these, offer insights into how you are valued in the relationship.

When you and your lover first met, you were shown nothing but respect. Your very presence used to captivate their attention and they used to hang on your every word. They used to care about how they looked around you so much that you never saw them when they weren't well-groomed. They used to think you were all that and a big bag of tortilla chips. If you've ever had it goin' on like this before, then you can truly say you know what it is like to be Top Dog in a relationship.

Stupid Pet Tricks

People who aren't Top Dog in their relationship and know it, tend to act in very humiliating ways. They know they're gettin' dogged out so they start doing stupid tricks to get the other person to love them again.

In Medieval times, there were people whose sole job was to do stupid tricks to make the rulers of the kingdom laugh. The king or queen being entertained only had one mandate: "Make me laugh or die!" How's that for pressure? Who would ever think that cracking somebody up could be a matter of life and death? This early comedian was called by many names. Sometimes he or she was called a clown, a court jester, and last but not least, a fool. It was no mistake that they used to call them fools, because only a fool would regularly bet his life on how funny he could be under life-threatening situations. If you allow someone to force you to play the fool in a relationship, know that people don't actually love fools, clowns, or comedians.

81

They just laugh at them. Realize that you're only as good to them as your last joke.

6. You Start Getting Dogged Out In Public

Of all the warning signs of whether or not you're getting dogged out, this warning sign represents the most dangerous threat to the health of the relationship. When you see yourself being flagrantly disrespected in the public eye, it is impossible to pretend you have a good relationship. It's non-debatable. These signs show up more often the longer the couple is together.

To discover that you are considered damn-near a non-person by someone you love is a very bitter pill to swallow. Though everyone else can see the disrespectful things being done to you and can point them out, it's easier for you to stay in denial and find ways to explain it all away. This type of rationalizing can continue for years. Only a healthy shot of self-respect, no matter from where it comes, can offer a cure for your relationship ills.

It's a fact that people will experience only so much pain before they eventually either give up totally or decide to stand up for themselves. This pain cuts both ways in a relationship. The person who's being disrespected and the person who's doing the disrespecting ultimately act out their agony. These actions generally take the form of verbal assaults on the disrespected person, as well as complaints about them to friends, family, and anyone else who will listen. Face it, there are people in this world who would rather talk "about" you than, "to" you. Everything happens in sequence. First they dis' you at home, then they dis' you in front of friends and family, and finally they dis' you in public. You know the relationship is just about over when your lover violently argues with you in public to such an extent that you know they don't care who sees it.

There are certain unspoken rules of etiquette when two people who claim to care about each other argue. Pay attention to when, where, and how much these rules are broken. The more your arguments occur in front of people, the more on the skids your relationship is. Also realize that if you never have disagreements at all, it's probably a clue that someone is lying to themselves and hiding their true feelings about some things in the love affair. Of course, it could also mean that you've been blessed with a perfect relationship. In which case, you should use this book for a coaster or for entertainment purposes only.

Getting dogged out isn't fun, and there is never a good reason for mistreating people. During the course of a lifetime, rare is the person who avoids being mistreated by someone they love. Sometimes it's done intentionally. Sometimes it's done insensitively. And sometimes it's merely because one person decides they don't want the other person anymore, and would rather have someone else. Nevertheless, pain is a result of the dogging out that begins. There is no way to accurately predict who will try to dog you out. This is why you must be willing to take the steps necessary to ensure that you aren't mistreated. The truth is, you can only be dogged out to the extent you allow yourself to be dogged out. If you choose to stay in a relationship where you are being continuously badly treated, ultimately, you are choosing pain over possible pleasure. The fault is yours.

Years ago, Clint Eastwood starred in a western called The Outlaw Josey Wales. In this movie, Clint played an anti-hero cowboy who always attracted trouble wherever he went. In one scene, there was an abandoned dog that came up to him. Clint's way of showing his affection was to chew a huge pinch of tobacco and then spit on the dog's head. Apparently, the dog interpreted this as an act of love, because he then followed behind Clint wherever he'd go. It was always the same scenario, Clint would spit on the dog and the dog would follow. Are you that dog?

Chapter 5
Picking the Dog with the best Pedigree

It has been said that if you want fresh food, you should go to a grocer. If you want good financial advice, you should go to an accountant. Therefore, if you want good relationship advice go to someone who has a good relationship. It's true that we can learn many valuable lessons from a wide variety of sources. It can't be denied that sometimes you can learn what not to look for in a partner by paying attention to what someone who made a bad choice actually found. However, research into the love lives of individuals who have definitely picked winning mates reveals much about the choosing process that we all should take into account.

It's taken these people sometimes quite awhile before they could successfully determine what to look for in a mate. Most have run the same gauntlet as everyone else. They too have fell in love for misguided reasons, chose people based on shallow things while overlooking important character flaws, and picked people based solely on desperation. But of all the couples interviewed for this book, there is one factor that made the difference in them finally finding a person that was right for them: They realized that nothing is more crucial than picking someone who has integrity. Integrity, much like honor, is what makes a person still act like a good person when no one is looking.

In the beginning, attraction usually occurs as a result of something about the other person's personality that is found to be appealing. Stuff like the way a person's sense of humor disarms you, the way a person caringly touches you, or even something as surface as the way a person always introduces you as their "boyfriend" or "girlfriend"! While these things are lovely indeed, they aren't what is ultimately going to decide whether or not this relationship will fulfill you happily in the long run. Integrity is the gauge by which is measured how an individual will interact with you in a lifetime relationship. If you think of a relationship like a section of good farmland, then personality is like topsoil, while integrity is the bedrock.

This chapter offers six things to look for when picking a suitable person to have a relationship with. Keep in mind, these categories have absolutely nothing to do with superficial traits that may be important to you in making your choice. But, in contrast, this is a list of time-tested qualities that reveal the true nature of an admirable person, either male or female. No matter what your current relationship status is, being able to identify these qualities will enable you to really see whether or not your present love prospect is ready to be coupled with you in a lasting partnership.

1. Pick someone who has Emotional Freedom

Picking a good partner is a lot like picking a good dog. It's all a question of breeding. Knowing what characteristics you're looking for in either a mate or a dog is good data to have. Just this type of knowledge alone will help you in avoiding starting a relationship with people who are still rabid. As you know by now, Rabid Dogs should never be fed, petted, or played with until they've had their shots.

Don't deceive yourself, a close relationship is not really cemented by sticking two people together under the same roof. It's really a product of compatibility. The compatibility we're concerned with at this point is in the area of emotional freedom. A person who has the ability to talk about their feelings, talk about your feelings, and talk about how you feel about each other. When you're strung out on someone, it's amazing how resourceful you can be when it comes to manufacturing reasons why you stay with people who aren't really there emotionally. But there always comes a time when you have to decide if you can live more comfortable with your excuses than you can without real emotional sharing. Let's be honest, if your lover can't open up to you about their feelings, then they're not emotionally free to hook up with you in any real way.

Hands down, emotionally free men and women are easily as giving with their feelings as a millionaire philanthropist is with his money. In the dog world, emotionally free people are like those dogs you see all the time that are always in the company of their master. Whether playing, barking, sleeping, or eating, these dogs do it all unashamedly in the presence of their master. They have nothing to hide. Likewise, emotionally free people are open and honest about the things they feel. With unbridled generosity, they share their emotions wholeheartedly and without reservations. In other words, these lovers are not shy about showing and telling you how much they love you when it's appropriate. They don't relegate their openness only to special occasions, or when they're intoxicated, or when you threaten to kick them to the curb for the thirteenth time. Now is the time to decide that you are entitled to have someone willing to love you without holding back.

Having someone in your life who is emotionally free allows you a doorway into their life that would remain closed otherwise. In this manner, they are giving you a personal tour of their private life. When a couple successfully makes a connection on a level this deep, only then can it be truly said that two can become one.

2. Pick someone who has Self-Respect

The amount of respect a person shows for him or her self is a determining factor in how much respect they show you. A killer oversight that we often make is picking people only according to how they treat us, but not noticing at all how they treat themselves. It's unfortunate, but many people who will go out of their way to show you love, ironically don't love themselves at all. People who have very little respect for themselves are more prone to be either too accommodating or extremely disrespectful to you. The flip side is also true, in that people who know respect are more apt to show respect. It's unlikely that a person who doesn't respect him or herself will be able to respect you. In a way, those who lack respect for themselves and others fit into the category of the Junkyard Dog. Remember, Junkyard Dogs are types of individuals that have personalities that are driven by their disregard and irreverence toward both themselves and others.

The more self-respect your ideal lover has, the better your relationship will be. Self-respecting people have a good idea of who they are. They think highly of themselves without crossing the line over into arrogance. People like these find contentment with who they are now and who they'll be in the future. Theirs is not a foolish pride born from conceit, but a quiet sense of assurance that comes from self-confidence. The more people respect themselves, the better they treat themselves. It can't be argued that the more you love yourself, the more you'll take a better care of your mind, body, and spirit. There's no way you can really love yourself and treat yourself disrespectfully at the same time. You can usually tell what people think of themselves by noticing how they take care of themselves and their possessions. Not to take this to extremes, but eating the right foods, exercising, and taking good care or your material things is a good indicator of your level of self-respect.

People with a good self-concept are not turned on by abuse or mistreatment. They don't lay down and take it when people try to dog them out.

Doggietales: Matthew, age 41:

I used to be one of those men who was willing to put up with anything just to have a woman in my life. Now, I didn't say I did it to have a "good" woman, I said "a" woman. As years go by, though, you get smart enough to know you can do better than that. I made a decision when I was 32. I decided I'd never keep dating any woman who refused to treat me the way I deserve to be treated. I treat women with respect, and that's how I expect to be treated. If I didn't get what I was looking for from a woman's treatment toward me, I stopped dating them. Now, I'm married with 3 beautiful girls. My life has been blessed because I found a woman willing to give love and respect, and not just to be on the receiving end. She was worth the wait.

Always keep in mind, self-respect is what makes a person refuse to let other people force-feed them a lot of crap and disrespect. When it comes to mistreatment, they never just take it and swallow it. After all, even dogs don't eat everything somebody puts in front of them. And they NEVER eat doo doo.

3. Pick someone who is pledged to personal development

Finding someone who is pledged to personal development is like finding a goldmine. Treasures abound for the person who finds someone who's dedicated to bettering themselves. If you find someone like this, you will have successfully side-stepped a variety of relationship traps certain couples fall into. Nothing is more vexing to one partner in a relationship like realizing that the other is not committed to personal growth.

Someone pledged to personal development is out to find out whatever they can about what it takes to grow into a better individual. This thirst for knowledge extends to a commitment to learning how to be a better mate or spouse. To have a person in your life who places a high priority on bettering themselves greatly increases your chances of having a smoother relationship. People big on self-improvement are more apt to be your ally in relationship rather than adversary. Being with someone who is at cross purposes with your relationship plan is a surefire way of shooting yourself in the foot.

For someone to be willing to accept outside assistance to better themselves is a big plus in any relationship. People too proud to ask for help are also too closeminded to be helped. It requires a certain degree of humility to open up to learning new things. Helpful influences can include anything such as the scriptures, clergy, tapes, seminars, counseling, or the advice of other couples in thriving relationships. It takes a humble man or woman who doesn't have a problem bowing in the presence of greater wisdom in order to learn. Relationships with people in them that don't know when to bend, break easily.

Someone with a pledge to personal development has actual plans for their own betterment. If you are a part of their lives for sufficient amount of time, their personal growth in specific areas can be charted. A lot of people like to engage in small talk about their big, life-changing plans, but how many of them really have the guts to stand up when it's time to do some death-defying? Taking up time running off at the mouth is one thing, but taking action is another thing altogether. Which brings us to the next important thing to look for when picking a dog with the best pedigree.

4. Pick someone who has wisdom and understands accountability

Some people, no matter how much you would like them to be, just are not good candidates for a serious love affair. If you are all about a "harmless" fling, they're okay. But, if you are looking for something more committed and fulfilling, you'd better look somewhere else. These folks may be very affectionate and head-over-heels "in love" with you, but they often lack the maturity necessary to sustain the amount of maturity needed to be accountable in a relationship.

People who are Golden Retrievers (as discussed in an earlier chapter) really need to be wary about picking lovers who are not wise and accountable. You hire yourself out as nothing more than cheap labor when you take the job of making someone else grow up. Usually, you'll only succeed in working yourself to death. It's better to quit, then find yourself a job you'll really like.

Those who are wise and understand accountability are also responsible. Being accountable means being a man or woman of your word. It means being aware and receptive of the fact that "the buck stops here". Accountability is what drives people to be on time for appointments, pay their car notes, and keep their relationship priorities straight. A good, decent human being to share your life with is one who is wise enough to be accountable for their own actions. Only folks who act like kids refuse to take responsibility for their actions. Therefore, it's always best to pick someone who is appropriately grown up inside and out to have a mature relationship with.

Doggietales: Denora, age 35:
Child, you should have met me before I got married. When I was single, if anybody was throwing a party, I was in the house. And those cute little short dresses I used to wear got me all the attention I could handle. I used to wear this black, body dress that used to show every inch. I had a great body and I loved to show it off. Now that I'm married and have two little kids, some things I've had to change. I'm a more mature woman now than I used to be. I'm somebody's wife now. I already have me a man so I don't have to go to nightclubs to get attention. I get my attention the same place I like to give it; at home! I'm a mother now too, so I don't wear those "come and get me" clothes I used to wear all the time when I'm out with them. I'm very aware of how I present myself to other people because I know my kids are watching. Believe it or not, I'm a role model now by choice and I wouldn't have it any other way. I actually feel more like an adult now, and it feels good. But don't get me wrong though, I still have a great body that I love to show off. The difference now is that the only guy I'm trying to turn on is my husband. And based on that silly grin he always has on his face, I think I'm doing a good job.

5.   Pick someone who is honest

Honesty is vital in any relationship. A relationship built on lies will collapse everytime. A dishonest person often lies when they find it too unpleasant for them to speak the truth. On the other hand, knowledge that you can depend on your lover to be honest with you consistently can provide you with great peace of mind. Hooking up with a dishonest person though, will only cause you anxiety and keep you on edge. You never know when to believe them and when not to. You can never trust them. Knowingly staying in a relationship with someone you can't trust is the same as handing a knife to a slasher who has stabbed you before, and turning your back. People who are dishonest are like serial killers who habitually kill the intimacy in their relationships by cutting off the trust.

Honest people don't make a habit of lying to themselves. Those who lie to themselves easily often can do so only because they are so well practiced. Practice makes perfect, and good liars have a lot of experience. The thing about dishonesty is that it is contagious. If you are in a relationship with someone who lies to you, it won't be long before you start lying either to them or for them. You may start lying for them to avoid embarrassment that is sure to come from others discovering that you are being played for a fool. Furthermore, it's also true that people who lie to other people in your presence do nothing but cause you to respect them less. After all, if your lover lies so unashamedly to everyone else, what guarantee do you have that they are always telling you the truth?

Lastly, persons with honesty are more upfront than those who are not. They don't try to conceal areas of their life from you. They are not evasive when it comes to answering simple questions. They don't make you play guessing games unnecessarily. Always pick a person to love who's actions line up with their words. Only interview candidates who say what they mean and mean what they say. If the lover you pick is always truthful, then you'll never have a reason to distrust them.

Doggietales: Breanne, age 26:

If it's one thing I can't stand it's a liar. It seems like every guy I meet is a damn liar. I mean, it's ridiculous. Men today lie about anything. They lie to you about their girlfriends, their wives, their jobs, their age, and everything else. These busters out here even lie about stuff that don't even matter. I had a guy to lie to me about the kind of car he drove, even though he met me riding the bus! If it's one thing I can't stand, it's a liar.

94

6. Pick someone who has positivity

Positivity is an attribute that is needed in every stage of a relationship. A partner without a positive attitude towards life in general is a poor choice to make when it comes to pairing for longevity. Positiveness is that which is within a person that makes them emphasize all that is worthwhile, hopeful, good, and constructive. Constructive is a word to describe these people, because negative people are the exact opposite. No one tears you down like the destructive effects of partnering with negative people. What your momma always told you is true. It's a proven fact that birds of a feather flock together. Association does bring about assimilation. There is absolutely no way you can continue to hang around negative people without becoming a little negative about some things yourself. It's more to your advantage to unite with someone positive, because their uplifting influence will inspire you also to greater heights of positivity.

People who are positive are problem solvers, not people who wallow easily in self-pity. They know that they are alive for the purposes of making their own private little world a better place. They believe that there is a sliver lining inherent in every cloud. They try their best to always turn every hardship into a vehicle of opportunity to learn and grow from. Though they are not always successful, their attitude of gratitude is what inspires them to both hope for and work for, the best in a relationship with you.

Taking the trouble to look for these qualities in an ideal mate is undeniably a very smart thing to do. It is unnecessary and also unrealistic to think that all these characteristics need to exist in the person in equal parts. Nobody's perfect, including you. Everybody is a mixed breed, somewhat. What this chapter is designed to do is to help you avoid those men or women who are straight-up mutts.

Dogs with the best pedigree areTop Dogs who are skilled at doing a great balancing act. They know which facet of their personality that is appropriate to exploit at any given time.

To everything in a relationship, there is a season.

And to everything in the life of a romance, there is a time and place:

A time to hunt, and a time not to hunt;

A time to show, and a time to not show;

A time to be sensitive, and a time not to be;

A time to tie, and a time to untie;

A time to be hot, and a time to be cool;

A time to be good, and a time to be good to yourself.

Therefore, the way to recognize a Top Dog, the dogs with the best pedigree, is by the way in which they leash and unleash each given facet of their personality according to the situation at hand.

Chapter 6
Dogcatcher's Tips

Becoming a good dogcatcher is always more a matter of skill than it is dumb luck. If you're one of those fortunate ones who has managed to stumble and fall into the relationship of a lifetime, then more power to you. However, most people aren't that lucky. True love hasn't hit them on the head yet, and they know they can't count on it happening anytime soon, either. That's where these strategies, these Dogcatcher's Tips come in handy. These dating tactics are not meant to be abusive or manipulative. Instead, these strategies are meant to be constructive toward getting you the type of person you want. The Dogcatcher's Tips will aid you in catching and keeping the "dog" you want. Although no plan is foolproof, these strategies compiled from researching people who have success in dating, represent your best chances for getting the relationship you want.

This may come as a shock, so brace yourself: PEOPLE LOOK FOR RAESONS NOT TO GET TO KNOW YOU! There can be no denying that everyone, including yourself, is looking for specific things in another person before they decide to get with them. As unfair as it may seem sometimes, unless you meet these narrow criteria that the person doing the picking has set, you are quickly disqualified. Getting the person you want to want you is a lot like interviewing for a much-coveted job. The preparation process is very similar. It's all about marketing who you are to convince the person in the decision making position that you are the best one for the job. You are, in effect, selling yourself. It is true that you never get a second chance to make a first impression. This is why the importance of putting your best "self" forward cannot be overstated. The aggravating part of all of this is that no matter what you know you have to offer the person you're pursuing on a deeper level, you'll never get an opportunity to show them if they reject what they see on the outside. Nobody is ever eager to rip open a present that they feel is not attractively gift wrapped. You must make yourself as seductive as possible. You must be inviting .

This is why it is not enough to just "be yourself". You've got to be the best "you" you can be. You've got to be yourself to the "nth" degree.

Sure, it's possible to meet the love of your life by just letting them find you, but research shows it's better to hunt. But, if you are one who is adamant about refusing to do your own shopping then you can at least prepare yourself as a package. There are four things that emerge from all the individuals interviewed that are determining factors in their decision to date. You must have The Look, The Confidence, The Fire, and The Focus.

The Look

The look has absolutely nothing to do with who you are, but how you appear. It is a very superficial criteria by which to judge someone, but it is a harsh fact of life. The look criteria doesn't necessarily have to be met by having flawless beauty or being stunningly handsome. Thankfully, attractiveness is such a subjective thing that there is a place for everyone on the "Fine" scale. No matter who you are, there is something physically attractive about you in the eyes of someone. Some people like jeeps and some people like sports cars. What is important here is to determine what features you have that are most attractive and how to exploit them. The better you take care of yourself thru diet and exercise, the better you'll look. Everyone is different, wear the clothes and hairstyles that compliment you. Remember, what works for someone else may not always work for you. It is always better to be a trendsetter than a fad follower. Develop your own look by mixing existing styles that flatter your overall physical appearance. Dressing to impress is really about impressing yourself. Fashion fever is just like a real fever. When you go too far and the fever fades, you'll sometimes look in the mirror and won't know who you are. People who are too trendy often go to ridiculous lengths to keep up with every trend. When they are successful they often only succeed in looking just like everyone else. Thus, they get lost in the shuffle. Your goal is to be an individualist who has a flair and style that makes you stand out in any crowd.

The Confidence

Confidence is the engine that drives everybody's individual personality. Without confidence, it is impossible to "be all you can be". Having confidence is the same as having assurance. Having confidence means that you have a strong belief in yourself and your abilities. Confidence comes from knowing who you are and being comfortable with the knowledge.

Confidence is like the wind, it cannot be seen with the naked eye. No one can actually see the wind, but everyone can see the effects of the wind. So it is with confidence. The way a person carries themselves provides casual onlookers with enough information to determine whether or not that person has confidence. Given a certain amount of exposures to you, people can also tell just as easily when you don't have it. Think about it; Does anybody ever have to tell you when the wind is NOT blowing? People can tell when you are having a crisis of confidence. If you don't verbally put yourself down, you will communicate your discomfort thru fumbling and fidgeting. When you don't have confidence, people seem to be in a big hurry to get away from you. The more pompous and insensitive the object or your affection is, the more mercilessly they will dismiss you from their presence. In fact, it is mindboggling how insensitive people can be to someone whom they already know would give the world just to be with them.

Confidence is not something that comes with ease for many people. It is also area specific. It's possible to have great confidence in the way you look, but absolutely no confidence in the way you talk. The fact of the matter is, we gain confidence from remembering our past successes. It is built stone upon stone into a platform that enables us to elevate to new heights of accomplishment.

The people interviewed for this book had a lot to say about confidence. The most important suggestions culled from the minds of confident people are as follows: Focus on the areas you do feel confident about when you are trying to make a good impression. This usually acts as a stress reliever in otherwise tense situations because you are drawing comfort from thoughts about yourself that you find pleasing. The second suggestion is to simply fake it 'til you make it. This may sound like a flimsy or shallow strategy to use, but really it isn't. If you practice acting like you're "The Bomb" long enough, eventually even you will start to believe it. Remember, the initial way that people think about you is based on the image that you choose to present to them.

The Fire

The fire is another word for enthusiasm. Enthusiasm and fire have a lot in common; They both are catching! Enthusiasm is a sense of zeal or passion about something. It is an attitude of intensity or of eager interest. The fire is an inspiration that comes from within. It burns from the inside out with a warmth and a glow that invites others to bask in it. The fire can only burn brightly when it burns from the heart. Whether it's dating or mating, when your heart isn't in it, the other person can tell.

Everything you do should be done with enthusiasm. If you have no enthusiasm about dating someone, it'll show immediately. Never forget that not only is enthusiasm catching, but so is boredom. You know the man or woman you're interested in has felt your "fire" when they too get excited in our presence. Let's not be ridiculous though, it is unrealistic to think it's possible to be "on" all the time. However, it is within your power to be "on" enough to avoid turning someone you're interested in "off".

The Focus

How attentive are you when you are out on a date? Do you let the other person know they are your primary object of interest? Do you have a habit of checking your watch and looking everywhere else in the room but at the lady you're with? Or, do you sit at the table with the guy who brought you but keep our eyes on the door to see if someone "better" comes in? If any of these questions sound like some you could answer "yes" to, then you may have a focus problem.

What you focus on tells you, and the person you're with, what you really would rather be doing. There's no denying it, if your attention is focused everywhere else but on your date, you should question your initial attraction to them. Sometimes though, maintaining your focus on the person you're with is a matter of practice. There had to be a reason why you wanted to date this person in the first place. Remember what those reasons were and focus on them. You may be delighted to discover little qualities and nuances that person has that will make you even more enamored with them. The power of focus will help you to see the other person more clearly. If the person really does have what you are looking for in a lover and you fail to focus your attention on them you'll miss out. Everyone likes the idea of knowing somebody is really into them. If you want to receive attention from someone, the best chance you have of getting it is to give it yourself.

The four criteria listed as The Look, The Confidence, The Fire, and The Focus are all intertwined. Any one area operating without the benefit of the others is usually rendered useless. If you have The Look with no Confidence, you're like a gun with no trigger. Also, if you have The Fire without The Focus, you're like a loose cannon with no target. But when all four are working in unison, you're a lethal weapon!

1. Pick Your Dog

A lot of people labor under the false belief that meeting the right person will be an event that is so sensational that it will be accompanied by loud music from a marching band. Many are amazed to discover that real love often comes accompanied by a quiet, simple melody that is so subtle that those who aren't listening for it will seldom recognize it. Every couple with a great meeting story is not destined to be together forever. Many relationships that start with a bang often end with a whimper.

And just because you meet someone under ordinary circumstances doesn't mean you can't develop an extraordinary love affair! The Bible itself advises us not to despise new experiences with small beginnings. Decide today to become more proactive and less passive about what you allow to happen in your love life. Why wait for love to happen when you can help make it happen?

The formula for solving the problem of finding true love is as basic as setting your sights on someone you're interested in and executing whatever maneuvers necessary to gain their romantic interest. Never approach someone you have no real interest in. This is both cruel to the other person, and a stupid waste of your time that could be better spent on a real romantic interest. Dedicate your time staying in hot pursuit, not trivial pursuit. If you see someone you want, go after them with gusto. This can be done either openly or subtly depending on either your gender or circumstance. A feeble, half-assed approach to your love life only succeeds in getting you more than your fair share of loss and resentment in the end. Many are afraid to approach the people they find most attractive because they fear rejection. They believe they could never survive being rebuffed by someone they hold in high esteem or that they put on a pedestal. Never realizing that they too are a worthy individual with much to offer the right person in a relationship, they relegate themselves to a life of feeling constantly inadequate.

The way to escape this fate is to realize that everyday of your life is another opportunity to both give and get the love you want. And every time you respond to each opportunity with action, the greater your chances for success. Ask any professional gambler and they will tell you that everything in life is a numbers game. The law of probability dictates that no one who keeps trying their "luck" loses forever. If you stay in the "game" you will eventually be a winner.

Doggietales: Rhonda, age 34

All my friends tell me I should have been a librarian. All my spare time I spend reading. My house is full of books. A lot of my casual conversations are about books. Even the movies I like

103

to go and see are usually adaptations of great books I've already read. So I guess its no surprise that I knew early on that the guy I would end up with had to be a book lover too. Every spring and fall all the big publishers host big autograph parties that I always make plans to attend. One year, at one of those very parties, I met the man I'm married to today. Julian was a man I had met at a previous autograph party that really caught my eye. This time when I saw him, I made it my business to strike up a conversation with him about the book he was holding. It turned out that we had the same taste in books. That night, we exchanged phone numbers and eventually began to date. As time went on, Julian and I found that there was a lot we had in common. Inside of a year, I was sure that I loved him more than any man I had ever known. We shared a connection on so many levels that from that moment on, I couldn't imagine my life without him in it. Obviously, Julian must have felt the same way, because it wasn't too long afterwards that he asked me to marry him. The rest, as they say, is history. That was seven years ago, and we're still very much in love with each other.

The lesson to be learned from Rhonda is that opportunity is everywhere you look. The only thing necessary to avoid missed opportunity is that you simply open your eyes.

Getting the love you want should never be a matter of dumb luck. Creating true romance is more art than accident for those who are most successful at this endeavor. As your skill level increases you will be more ready to quickly seize the opportunity for any romantic encounter that may arise. The more you practice shooting the breeze with people you're interested in, the easier it will become. Before long, establishing rapports with desirable candidates for love will become easy and comfortable to you. If you're a man, you will be known by women as a man of the world. If you're a woman, you will be known by men as a woman for all seasons. Exploiting different facets of who you are should never be thought of as being fake. To the contrary, it should only be considered as appropriate behavior for the appropriate circumstance or occasion. After all, men of the world are so worldly because of their ability to make their words revolve around whatever the appropriate subject is for that moment. And women for all seasons are who they are because of their ability to change their conversation to fit their environment.

2. Keep Your Dog Barking

Let's say you've set your sights on someone you really want to get with. Your main goal is to find out as much about them as you can. It is the custom of some to get info about someone they're attracted to from other people. This is an okay strategy to use in the absence of any really first hand knowledge, but information gathered directly from the source is usually much more reliable. Keep your dog barking is another way of saying keep your date talking. Going on a date is not like going on a tour, it's more like going on a hunt. Whether it'll turn out to be a scavenger hunt or a treasure hunt is something that only time will reveal. Why all this talk about comparing dating to hunting and digging for information? Prepare yourself for another major shock: PEOPLE GO OUT ON DATES TO GET TO KNOW YOU, NOT FOR YOU TO GET TO KNOW THEM! The whole trick to dating is to get the other person to keep talking while you pay close attention to what is being said. People tell you a lot about themselves by what they say, as well as by what they don't. If you stay alert, they'll tell you what they believe spiritually, what they're interested in personally, and what they like and don't like. Everyone has certain strengths and weaknesses to their character. We all have our fair share of eccentricities and idiosyncrasies that make us the people we are. Common sense should tell you that the more you know about someone, the better you're able to establish a meaningful rapport.

Subject Matters

"Macks" and "players" will quickly tell you that there is no such thing as a corny line, if it works. These "experienced" men and women know that anything said with a straight face and a tone of sincerity has a good chance of working. But beyond rehearsed lines, corny or otherwise, it is always true that we're

105

more preoccupied with ourselves than we are with anybody else. This isn't necessarily so much a narcissistic thing as it is a natural thing. We as human beings are filled with such a wide variety of thoughts and emotions that it's no wonder that it takes another individual with an intrinsic understanding of this to capture our attention. As a result of this tendency in us all, the only way possible to really get on the same wavelength with someone you're just meeting is to actually take an interest in them. True communication is not a matter of meaningless chatter, but rather a connection that results from the sharing of ideas. Communication is an even exchange. It is a two-way street. The two sides involved should take turns talking and listening. The odds of getting someone's attention are dramatically increased if you say things that play to their interests. Ask any politician and they'll tell you that no one will give you the time of day unless you tell them what they want to hear first. At the start of every conversation when you're trying to endear yourself to someone whom you find attractive, you must first find a way to smash thru their barrier of initial disinterest. These barriers that so many people have around them can seem incredibly cold and hard as you're trying to get thru. Congratulations, now you know why they call it "breaking the ice".

One of the worst things you can do when initiating a conversation with someone is to go into it already assuming you know what type of person the object of your desire is. The absolute worst thing you can do is pigeonhole them to such an extent that you only talk to them about subjects that you feel may fit whatever preconceived stereotype you may have. It's easy to assume that an athlete only wants to talk about his favorite sport or a doctor only wants to talk about her medical practice. However, many times, this really isn't the case at all. Remember, you and everyone else has many different sides to their identities. The more well-rounded their personality, the more they can talk about. This is why it's wise to sometimes play detective and uncover clues to the interests of the person you're talking with.

Second to themselves, people really get a lot of pleasure out of talking about other people. Women call it gossip. Men like to

106

call it keeping each other up on what's going on. Whatever you want to call it, the one thing that's certain is that everybody does it. Ironically, it doesn't matter if the things that are said about the person being discussed is true or not. It's the very act of talking about other people's lives that we as human beings find so fascinating. Depending on your point of view, this can be a positive thing. For the clever conversationalist, there is a way to accentuate the positives of the person in question without contradicting the particular point of view of the person you're talking with. Even if you're unsuccessful in steering the "gossip" into something positive, at least you have succeeded in keeping them continuously talking to you.

Another thing people like to do in the company of others is to share their personal points of view. Everyone gets a certain amount of enjoyment from expressing their opinions on a variety of subjects. One thing's for certain: No matter how substantive or how slight, everyone believes their opinions are important. The subjects that people will talk about are without limit. It is very important that you don't miss this opportunity to pay attention to detail. Good listeners have learned to like listening because of all the things they can learn. Everyone has a little trouble bending an ear to listen to something that they initially care little about. This is normal and human. However, it is also normal for anyone to find themselves becoming engrossed in the oddest of subjects once their interests have been piqued. Besides, a great by-product of listening to someone talking about a subject you know nothing about is that you are geometrically expanding your own ability to speak on a wide variety of subjects. In other words, the more you learn from one conversation, the more you can contribute to another.

Something that is absolutely true, but hard to admit, is that many of us sabotage any chance we have of having a meaningful conversation by talking about ourselves too much. Let's keep it real. The truth is that people don't want to listen to our sob stories, our pessimistic points of view, or our personal bad news reports. These types of conversations are major turnoffs. You should never beat people over the head with depressing stuff like this when you first meet them. You should wait and get to know

107

them for a couple of days, then do it! But seriously folks, don't allow yourself to fall into the habit of whining to people you don't know. To someone meeting you for the first time, it makes a horrible first impression. It is always better to share your deep, inner feelings about your trials and tribulations with family and longtime friends. These are people who already love you unequivocally. Don't alienate a new romantic prospect by bringing them down every time you open your mouth. If you watch what you say, you won't recklessly give the other person a reason to write you off. Remember, people look for reasons NOT to go out with you.

It's usually a good idea to keep your conversation revolving around either the subject or the person you're talking with. Letting the other person get a word in edgewise is necessary for an equally balanced exchange of ideas. This easy give and take, this verbal changing and exchanging, is the goal of any good conversation. Only an egomaniac wants to talk about his or herself all the time. If you're patient, and the other person does ask you about yourself, you'll then undoubtedly have their undivided attention. When you are speaking during the conversation, it's usually a waste of time if you choose to focus only on yourself. It's always more advantageous to use this as a chance to link your interests with the other person's in order to establish a stronger rapport.

Be positive in the things you say to others. Be the type of person who uplifts others and enlivens any conversation. Association historically is proven to bring about assimilation. If you're upbeat in your conversations with people, you'll increase your chances of them being upbeat around you. Realistically, there are times when you just don't feel happy and enthusiastic about life. What should you do when you feel this way? The answer is to act as if you are! This may sound silly, but over a period of time this can really work for you. Except for extreme cases of depression, the more positive you act, the more positive you will eventually feel. The more you focus on things in your life that lift your spirits, the more uplifting your overall conversations will be.

Never be afraid to make the first move. It's easy to talk yourself out of striking up a conversation with a complete stranger. After all, wasn't one of the first bits of advice that our parents gave us was that we shouldn't talk to strangers? Seriously, if we followed this childhood advice to the extreme as adults, we'd never meet anybody. The truth of the matter is that all our friends, lovers, and acquaintances would have remained strangers if someone hadn't first broken the ice. If you're serious about meeting the kind of person you've always wanted to be a part of our life, that ice breaker has to be you. The successful couples interviewed for this book have stated that smiling always offers a good starting point. A nice, easy smile at the right time can be a good indicator to the other person that you may be a candidate for a pleasant conversation. The best way to start any conversation is to ask a question. Preferably the questions asked should be open-ended rather than closed-ended. Never ask a question of a man or woman that they can give a one word answer to. More often than not, they will choose this "yes or no" option out of either initial disinterest or plain old nervousness. If you choose to ask closed-ended questions you are at the mercy of whether or not the other person wants to elaborate. Don't give them a choice. By asking questions that are open-ended, questions that lend themselves toward more detailed answers, you are extending the conversation and getting the other person more involved. On the other hand, open-ended questions shouldn't be so broad that they are overwhelming or intimidating. Keep in mind, this is not an episode of NYPD BLUE or LAW AND ORDER, so there's no need to come across as a bad cop. This is a casual conversation, not a questioning or an interrogation. A first meeting is usually not the right time to ask someone what their take on the meaning of life is. It's best to start off by asking the person less invasive questions either about them or about whatever matter that may be at hand. The less threatening the question, the more comfortable the other person will be in answering. People are more relaxed when you ask them "little" questions. Folks might chat with you all day if you start by asking them "tiny" questions. Now you're beginning to get the idea why they call it "small" talk.

Third Date Abracadabra

Doggietales: Floyd, age 34

When I first met Charice I thought she was it. Charice was the total package, you know. Charice had brains, class, and sexiness. The first date we had was very hot. Just being in her company was a turn-on. The second date was kind of smooth, too. Everything was going fine like the first date, except I noticed how she talked down to the waitress who was serving us at the restaurant. I really didn't appreciate how she gave that poor lady so hard a time just because the chef was a little slower than usual. See, that was the first time I really paid attention to how she could sometimes be insensitive towards other people whenever she couldn't have things exactly her way. By the time we went on our third date, little selfish things Charice was doing really started to work my nerves. Not only was she being mean to the valet who parked the car, she even had the nerve to start criticizing and making sarcastic comments about my driving skills on the way back from the casino. With me being the kind of man I am, I quickly let her know that she could keep her smart-assed comments to her damn self. It's no surprise that after that, it was a long ride back to our part of town. As I was dropping her off, it occurred to me that I almost couldn't remember what it was about her that made me ask her out in the first place!

Doggietales: Tracie, age 27

Let me tell you about how I got hooked up with Stan. Stan was the last guy I thought I'd ever get with. Anybody who knows anything about me, also knows that Stan is definitely not my type. I'm sure you probably know girls just like me. I guess I'm your typical "pretty girl". I was very outgoing in high school. I was very popular. I was voted most attractive because I had the best figure. I always got the best guys. Now here I am ten years later and I've still got it going on!

I recently went back to my high school reunion and there was Stan. Stan was always a cute guy, but back than he was a little shorter and kind of square. Stan hadn't really changed that much since back in the day. True, he was a little taller and his cuteness had graduated to handsomeness, but my opinion of him was still the same. At the reunion, on a whim, I gave Stan my number and we went on our first date. Just as I thought, Stan really came across as nice as I remember, but also just as square. During our date, Stan had no trouble telling me how strongly he had always felt toward me, and also how strongly he felt toward his career. As it turned out, Stan was the owner of a small, but growing cartoon production company. At the time of our first date, he had just released his first completed project on home video. It was a story about a little boy who grew up in a bad neighborhood, moved out, made it big, then came back to help his family and community. You see I know so much about it, because it was almost all Stan talked about the whole time. Now I like a good story as much as the next girl, but I was bored to death. So bored that it took Stan almost a month of asking before I finally "freed" my calendar enough to go out with him again. I hate to admit it now, but the only reason I went out with Stan again was because I was having a slow dating period. Anyway, on our second date, I started to see a whole new side to Stan. I began to take note of just how open he was to sharing his emotions with me and also how open he was to doing new things. On this second date, Stan surprised me by agreeing to come to a company Christmas party with me. Not only was "square" Stan comfortable in a party atmosphere, he was the life of the party! Stan danced me until I couldn't dance anymore! We had a real good time that night. After our date, as I stood in the shower, I found myself thinking of Stan in a very different way. My third date with Stan was the one that put it all together for me. He had asked me to meet him at a local video store where he was making a special appearance to promote is video release. As I walked in, I hung in the background a while and watched him sign his video for the fans. I watched as parents and kids told him how much they liked and appreciated his work. I could tell by the look on his face that Stan was more than just "happy" that his work had such a positive effect. He was thrilled. This was not just business to him, it was passion! it was this passion that filled his life that made me see him in a whole new way. I never thought I could go for a guy who wasn't flashy, but Stan changed all that. On that date, I began to recognize qualities in Stan that I really like. To this day, I can't tell you how glad I am I did myself a favor back when I decided to go out with him again.

Floyd and Tracie have both found themselves assisting in a magic trick that happens in every new relationship. It's called Third Date Abracadabra. This is the name given to describe the process that occurs when fantasy gives way to fact. It is the moment when you notice that the person you're dating has started to transform into who they really are. This rule isn't set totally in stone, but usually by the time of your third date you start to see the object of your desire as a real person. It's true, no matter how idealized the mask you put on your dream guy or gal, it's generally cracking by the third date.

The most interesting thing about Third Date Abracadabra is that it is completely unpredictable. There is really no way to tell in advance how you will feel about a person until you actually spend time with them. In Floyd's case, Third Date Abracadabra magically transformed his lady into someone more unattractive. But in Tracie's case, her guy was magically changed into someone more attractive. In a way, this phenomena is a lot like the intro to the old Rocky and Bullwinkle cartoon. Each show would start with Bullwinkle the moose performing a magic trick where he would pull something out of the hat. The joke was that no matter what Bullwinkle said he was going to pull out of the hat, he always surprised himself and everybody else by pulling out something completely different. The moral of this story is that you never know what you're getting when you first meet someone. But, you will begin to get an idea by the third date. This seems to have a strong element of truth to it since cursory interviews indicate that people rarely have a fourth date with people they don't like. In other words, if you find yourself on a fourth date with someone it's usually because you feel they're worth getting to know better. No one spends four or more dates

113

with someone unless there is a perception of a chance to build something special. It is essential at this point in getting acquainted that you find pleasure in the other person's company. Anything less than this would be equal to hard labor. Dating then would have changed from play to work. We all would rather play than work any day. If people equate dating you with going to a job they hate, then they'll soon stop "working" with you and go find themselves a new "play" mate. Remember, people as a rule rarely look forward to their next work day, just their next day off!

3. Bury Your Bones In Plain Sight

Burying your bones in plain sight is the Doggiestyle way of saying get yourself a good PR campaign going. PR of course, is short for pubic relations. A public relations campaign can be defined as that part of your dating mission that focuses on creating a very favorable opinion of yourself in the eyes of the person you want. This concept is definitely one that has a lot in common with marketing. However, it is more akin to free publicity than it is to paid advertising. Studies have shown that the average person has an aversion to blatant advertising, but not publicity. This is why a hard sell is usually a turn-off, while a soft sell is a turn-on.

When it comes to creating ways for the person you want to see you favorably, there are two strategies. Either you can bury your own bones in plain sight or you can get someone else to do it.

The Multiplicity Effect

If you are one who prefers to do your own public relations work in new relationships, know that your ultimate goal is to create the Multiplicity Effect. For those who don't know, the Multiplicity Effect is a concept that was inspired by the hit movie that came out awhile back called Multiplicity. In it, Michael Keaton plays a man with a very busy and complicated life. Thru the results of a scientific experiment, he comes up with the perfect way to simplify his life: He decides to clone himself. This way, he thinks, he'll finally have enough of himself to go around. What a far-fetched movie concept, you may say. But think of it, wouldn't you really like to have another "you" by your side helping you achieve your goals? Alas, since Multiplicity was just a movie, this is literally impossible. But, thanks to the creation of the Multiplicity Effect, it is now figuratively possible! The Multiplicity Effect is the phenomena that occurs when you manage to occupy two places at once. This is done by finding ways to make the person you're dating think about you even when you're not there. There are a variety of ways to accomplish this, but the best way is to give the person you're pursuing "meaningful" gifts or mementos. A memento isn't a gift that is necessarily expensive, but it is certainly not trivial. The worth of the gift has nothing to do with monetary value. Instead, it is a souvenir that serves as a reminder of either how special you are, or how special you two are together.

Doggietales: Andre, age 30

My brother was in town to be at our cousin's wedding the night I met Laurene. I know it was a long time ago, but I still remember it like it just happened. We had just checked out the movie Soulfood, and it made us so hungry we just had to stop by my favorite restaurant and get us something to eat. As soon as we got there, we found out a lot of people had the same idea. It was so crowded that it was standing room only until you could get a table. Me and my brother Ricky were standing there talking about how hungry seeing that movie made us when I overheard two girls standing in front of us talking about the same thing. Because they were so close to us, we struck up a conversation with them. We all seemed to hit it off real well right away. Especially Laurene and I. Laurene was about five foot two with a nice shape and a friendly personality. All of us were getting along so well that we decided to just get a table together. By the time we left, Laurene and I had exchanged numbers and addresses because we wanted to see each other again. The week after I met Laurene, I got the idea of special delivering a gift-wrapped, Soulfood CD to her because I remembered how much she said she liked the music in the movie. That was quite a while ago, and to this day Laurene still tells me that everytime she plays that CD she thinks about me.

Andre is a smart man. Instinctively he knew that giving Laurene that CD as a memento was the same as him finding a way to be in two places at one time. Andre was not content with just resting on the strength of his first impression. He wanted to double his impact. So he "multiplied" himself.

The Doggy Bag Effect

On the other hand, if you're the type of person who prefers to let others do your public relations for you, then creating the Doggy Bag Effect is what you should be going for.

For the benefit of those who have never been unable to finish a meal at a restaurant, a doggy bag is another name for leftovers. Doggy bags are what we liked to call the containers that we take home from the restaurant because we wanted to feed them to our dogs. Eventhough we still call them that, everybody knows that we take these leftover goodies home and eat them ourselves. They are our guilty pleasures.

The trick to burying your bones in plain sight in this case is to find ways to do things that show you in a positive light while the right people are watching. Who are the right people? These people can be your prospect's friends, family, or associates. Anyone whom he or she thinks well of will do for this purpose. These individuals are messengers whose jobs it is to deliver good reports of all your doings and sayings to the person you are trying to get with. Do things in the presence of people he or she knows that you know will impress them once they hear about it. Say nice things about the person you're dating to his or her friends, simply because you know that it'll get back to them. The key to this whole strategy is to keep it real subtle. It's entirely possible to be impressive without being overly expressive. You can put on a show without showing out, and you can have a talk without talking too much. Exercise a little restraint and you will be rewarded for your efforts with good reports. Getting other people to hand your romantic interest doggy bags is a great way to leave them with tasty, leftover, morsels of you that will have them thinking of you even when you aren't there.

However, the best way to successfully bury your bones in plain sight is not to use either the Multiplicity Effect or the Doggy Bag Effect, but to use both. For the sake of argument, let's say that winning the affections of someone you're interested in is a lot like playing in a NBA championship game. If the Multiplicity and Doggy bag strategies are like the last two free throws you can take to win the game, would you take just one? Enough said.

4. Play With Your Dog

Playing with your dog is the Doggiestyle way of advising you to spend lots of great moments with the person you're trying to get to know better. Couples who have managed to happily stay together over a long period know that love is a constant revelation. Time reveals all. There really is no other way to actually get to know a person better than to spend time with them. How will the other person know what an amazingly wonderful catch you are if they can barely catch up with you? Your strategy is to make yourself available for worthwhile engagements. In this case, as in many others, quality outweighs quantity. There is much to be said for the cumulative effect of constantly being together, but this must be handled carefully. If you're not around enough, you run the risk of not being there enough to keep them captivated. On the other hand, if you're always there, you can ruin the image the other person has of you by overexposure. You've heard it said that absence makes the heart grow fonder. If there is any shred of truth to this, and you're constantly crowding them, they'll never miss you because you're always around. The answer is for you to be mindful of how much time you spend with the object of your desire. You should make every effort to control both the frequency of your encounters and how you want to come across during these encounters.

A good way to play with your dog is to make your date's areas of interest yours. If burying your bones in plain sight is the same as sowing the seeds of love, then playing with your dog can be considered similar to growing your crops. Making someone else's interests your own can be advantageous in several ways. If you're a gifted enough actor or actress, you will succeed in convincing the person you're dating you really do have a lot in common. That's fine if you want to feel like you're on stage the whole relationship, but thankfully there's another way you can go with this strategy. The better alternative is to genuinely make his or her interests your own. It's not unheard of for people to develop a real interest in hobbies or past times that they were introduced to by the person they're dating. This could happen to you, if you can manage to keep an open mind. It's really a matter of how much you like the other person. Is this lady or gentleman worth the trouble of taking the time to sample some things in their lives that they find enjoyable? Only you can answer that question. Only you can determine your level of interest.

The quality of any loving relationship today is composed of all the good memories they've made over time. The events you attend together, the trips you take together, and even the idle time you spend together are more important to the future of your relationship than you realize. Make the times you spend with your new love prospect as pleasant as you can, because when today becomes yesterday you'll want their memories to be good ones

5. Pet Your Dog and Give'm Plenty of Scooby Snacks

Dog lovers are very familiar with the philosophy behind petting your dog and giving out plenty of scooby snacks. Petting a dog is the same as rubbing and stroking him or her. There is a time and a place for everything. When you find yourself in a relationship with a promising new person you've been dating, your main priorities are to reinforce the behaviors in them that you like and punish those that you don't. Keep your eyes open.

118

Knowing when to reward your partner and when to discipline them is a skill that you will develop as things progress.

Scooby Snacks

Anyone who grew up in the seventies, or who has ever watched cable television's Cartoon Network, without a doubt remembers Scooby Doo. Scooby Doo was a show about a gutless dog who was the mascot for a team of teenage detectives. Whenever those young sleuths needed Scooby's help on a case, they knew they had to give him a Scooby Snack. For their purposes and ours, a Scooby Snack is a reward for a job well done. The strategy is simple. Whenever your new love acts in any way that pleases you, find a special way to "reward" him or her for this good behavior. After you've been with someone long enough, you've learned enough about them to know things that you can do for them that will really make their day. A Scooby Snack can be anything from giving them an impromptu back rub or a brand new car. Like the aforementioned memento, a Scooby Snack needn't be a big financial expenditure. A Scooby Snack can be a word, a gesture, or a nice, warm bath. The choice is yours. In fact, it is a good idea to get in the habit of always "stroking your new love behind the ears" for practical reasons. Your best chance for receiving affection is to give it generously. Affection, in and of itself, should be given freely throughout a romance anyway. Would you stay with someone who knew how to keep you happy all the time but refused to? If you have good sense, your answer is "no". That's why it's critical to point out the difference between affection and Scooby Snacks. Affection is free, Scooby Snacks are a reward you give to your lover for being exceptionally loving towards you.

If you want to train your new love to keep pleasing you in a specific area, make sure you reward them handsomely everytime they do it. Don't take any kind act done toward you for granted. Leave no good deed left unrewarded. Know that the more you show your appreciation, the quicker you'll change their behavior into habits you like.

119

So how do you bring your ideal lover into you life? Follow the Dogcatcher's Tips:

1. Pick Your Dog
2. Keep Your Dog Barking
3. Bury Your Bones In Plain Sight
4. Play With Your Dog
5. Pet Your Dog and Give'm Plenty of Scooby Snacks

Are the Dogcatcher's Tips a written guarantee for relationship success? No.

Do the Dogcatcher's Tips work on every man and woman you meet? No.

Do the Dogcatcher's Tips have a high success rate based on the experiences of people who have lasting, loving relationships? The answer is a resounding YES! They represent the best strategies available for helping you find and keep the love in your life that you've always wanted. Put these strategies to work for you, and dare to change your love life for the better forever!

Chapter 7
Walking The Dog: Keepin'em on a Short Leash vs. a Long chain!

So now that you've purchased that doggie in the window, how do you keep him or her for yourself? The simple answer is that what won them initially will continue to win them. By now, it should be evident that good relationships aren't born, they're made. Love at first sight can't generate perpetual passion. Love at first sight can't continuously create compatibility. Love at first sight cannot sustain even an already good relationship. Only a willingness to work at keeping your romantic relationship fresh can maintain it's quality. This is why the "doggie" you picked out of the window must be worthy of your time and effort.

Keeping your dog on a short leash vs. a long chain is a very important choice to make when it comes to walking your dog. Walking the dog is a phrase used to picturize the process of going out in public with your new love. Keeping them on a short leash versus a long chain refers to how firm or relaxed a grip you hold on your partner when you're out in public. First of all, let us quickly do away with even the notion that keeping your lover on a short leash is even an option. Controlling someone's life to the point where you have to know their every move is neurotic. Obsessing over your new love's whereabouts is a surefire way to mentally run yourself ragged. There isn't a person in the world who loves the idea of being kept on a short leash by a person who "claims" to care about them. The thought alone of being on a short leash brings to mind images of confinement. Unless your new love interest is in fact, a convict, then this notion of a "penitentiary" kind of love is a bad idea. To keep somebody on a short leash is to, in effect, put them on lockdown. If you plan on keeping the new lady or gentleman you're dating in your life by using these kinds of tactics, then be aware that this is extremely risky behavior. Consider this: When you imprison your innocent lover like a convict, you put yourself in the role of

121

warden. And if your love suddenly becomes a prison, can a jailbreak be far behind?

Dogs Can Smell Fear

When you have finally met someone you are excited about, there is usually a strong temptation to fall prey to anxiety. It seems somehow normal to let yourself sink into the waters of worry from time to time. Bowing to fear is like believing a mirage. Allowing yourself to be paralyzed by fear is the same as accepting the illusion of your worst-case romantic scenario as reality. In this light, it can be clearly seen how fear is the evil mirror image of faith. Actually, it all really boils down to a personal choice. It takes just as much energy to believe the best as it does to believe the worst. To expect the best inspires you and motivates you to do your best. On the other hand, to expect the worst discourages you and only succeeds in bringing out the worst in both you and your relationship. It doesn't take a mathematical whiz to figure out which particular choice is the correct equation for peace of mind. Allowing yourself to be fearful of losing the other person all the time distracts you from doing the things that will keep them. The anxiety that you give off is perceptible to the other person. Dogs can smell fear, you know. And it will surely effect how they see you.

Doggietales: Everett, age 27

Chela was the baddest chick I had ever seen. We met almost a year ago while we were both in Atlanta in graduate school. Chela was from Florida, and so was I. We were both fish out of water, in a way. We always sat next to each other in class and got to know each other that way. She was a devastating combination in that she was as smart as she was fine. I guess it was because I was from her same hometown that I felt I could hook up with her. If my friends back home could have seen me then,they wouldn't have recognized me. I was suave. I was relaxed. I was confident. I mean, I was the man! You know what I mean? Things were good for us all while we were at the university. It was when we both finished and moved back home that it went downhill. I don't know what got into me. I already knew that Chela was all that when I met her, but it was something about being back in Florida that was shaking me up. I was scared she wouldn't want to be with me anymore since she was back on her old stomping grounds. I guess I just kind of lost it. I started asking her where she was going all the time, and who with. I even drove by some places where she said she would be just to see if her car was there. One time though, I saw her car parked in a secluded spot at an apartment complex where I knew her old boyfriend lived. I was pissed. I can remember just sitting there gripping my steering wheel tighter and tighter until I just couldn't stand it any longer. Since they were taking their time getting out of the car, I decided to go and confront them instead. I got out of my car and went up to Chela's window and said to her, "Oh, this is how you've been playing me?" Chela, in shock, just looked at me without saying a word. Just then, the passenger side door opened and out stepped Paula. Paula was an old friend of Chela's who recently moved back to Florida herself. The apartment complex where we were happened to be where she lived too. Chela hasn't spoken to me since.

Everett's story is a painfully clear picture of how fear can derail a relationship that could have actually gone somewhere. He was so afraid of losing Chela that he hadn't noticed until it was too late that he had lost himself.

The way you carry yourself in your lover's presence speaks volumes to everyone around you what you think of yourself. Everett's story is not rare. Many are the tales of deserving people who lose their chance at love thru lack of confidence. There is no good reason for you to add yourself to the statistic when you now have a set of strategies to guard against it.

Good Dogs Don't Beg

All relationships, no matter how solid, all reach something called the challenge stage. The challenge stage is that time in all romances where the strength of the relationship is put to the test. You know when you've reached the challenge stage when the person you're involved with starts distancing themselves from you. Now this usually doesn't occur abruptly. More often, this happens a little bit at a time. They used to call you every other day, but now it's every other week. They used to love having you around, but now they act like they don't want you anywhere near them. You used to have trouble keeping your hands off each other, but now you're noticing you're the only one doing the reaching. As stated by these examples, there are a number of indicators that you have entered the challenge stage. However, more important than the stage itself, is what you do when you're in it.

The whole purpose of the challenge stage is to subtlety pose a couple of questions. The first question they're asking is, "How deep is your love?" The second is, "How free is your love?" These two questions are very important to anyone who has ever been in a relationship that lasts any length of time. The answers to these questions directly influence whether or not we decide to take the leap of faith from having a casual affair to having a serious romance. Both parties in a budding relationship require from the other answers to these burning questions. When taking into consideration human nature, this shouldn't seem hard to understand at all. Everyone is avidly in search of a sense of security in some form or another. Even though it can never literally really exist, wouldn't we all like a written guarantee that our love will last? Don't we all want to know whether or not someone really and truly cares about us? Wouldn't we all find comfort in the knowledge that our relationships would remain emancipating rather than suffocating? Now you know why the challenge stage is a rite of passage that all lasting romances go through.

When the person you really care about starts to pull away from you, the last thing you should ever do is beg. Begging translates into whining in the ears of someone who doesn't want to hear it. People find whiners to be annoying. When the man or woman of your dreams starts acting as if they want out of your life, never stoop to begging because it'll surely fall on deaf ears. Think about it: If they are having doubts about staying with you when your self-esteem is high, how attractive will a shameless display of low self-esteem make you?

More Mystery, Less History

When you find yourself faced with a challenge, it is crucial that you don't "play yourself". Never playing yourself means never revealing to your "distant" lover that you either know what they are doing or that you have a strategy to counteract it! It's well known that this is known as the information age, but there is still such a thing as too much information. To beg for relationship scraps from someone who used to give you their all is to teach them that you have a low opinion of yourself. It teaches them that you feel that you are lucky to have them. And that's giving them too much information. As stated in an earlier chapter, the answer is to fake it 'til you make it! It doesn't matter if you have to put on an Oscar caliber performance, just never beg them to stay. Instead of groveling and begging when your lover wants to leave, you must appear strong, self-assured, and equally unconnected. Your show of independence in the face of losing them represents your best chance at accomplishing two things: The first thing this strategy can do is to let the other person know that you are self-sufficient and that they can leave guilt-free. The second thing this strategy can do is change the question in their mind from how can they get out of the relationship to whether or not they really want to go! Although there are no entirely foolproof plans, it is not unusual for the person who at first wants out of a relationship to suddenly stop dead in their tracks when they discover that the person they're about to dump is unphased by the idea of their leaving. In a way, this is a big blow to the ego of the person who wants to leave. They are usually so busy at the time thinking about how much they want to leave you that it comes as quite a shock to them that you might also want to leave them! Just the realization alone that you can happily live without them can oftentimes hit them as devastatingly hard as a preemptive breakup! This is why you must never beg when faced with the possible loss of your ideal person's love. Your show of confidence in the challenge stage can make all the difference in whether or not your love will last. If you believe this person to be worth it, it is in both parties' best interest that you knowingly inject a little mystery into the relationship at the appropriate times. Otherwise, a once thrilling romance could gradually become ancient history.

Show'em Who's Master

It has often been said that the best defense is a good offense. Truer words were never spoken. To always be the best "you" you can be is the best strategy for having a great romance. As discussed in the previous chapter, strengthening yourself in the areas of your look, your fire, your focus, and your confidence are the best ways to go on the romantic offensive. You will need these, and every other weapon at your disposal, to maintain a winning relationship. The only way to keep showing your lover who's master is to keep practicing mastering yourself.

Getting Rid of Your Dog's Flea Problem

One thing to be on the lookout for after you've picked a "dog" you really like is the occasional pesky flea problem. It never fails, just when things are going extremely well, here comes yet another challenge to the longevity of the relationship. "Fleas" are another name for anybody who tries to attach themselves to your partner for the purpose of taking them away from you. Fleas can be either old boyfriends or girlfriends, or brand new people who are out to woo your partner away from you. It's an odd quirk of human nature that most people at some time or another fall prey to the temptation of wanting something just because they think they can't have it. This is how your new love's exes sometimes see them, once they find out you are the new Top Dog in their life. When faced with this new challenge, the offensive strategy is still the same. Every reaction you have and every move you make that comes from a foundation of high self-esteem and confidence is sure to fare you well in the face of any competition. It matters not whether your dog's Flea problem comes from someone old or new, you should never let fear of losing them dictate how you behave in their presence. If you find yourself feeling insecure or are having a crisis of confidence, the last thing you should ever do is let your partner know this. Never paint yourself as inferior in the eyes of someone with whom you're trying to establish a new relationship. Remember, people have a tendency to see you how they think you see yourself. Since yours is a new relationship, love is not fully formed yet and has attached to it many conditions. To come across as the exact same person of confidence you were when you met them should be your only concern during these times. If you feel the need to unburden yourself of all your fears and worries, don't call your lover because that's what friends are for. Instead of wasting your time worrying about whether or not your blossoming relationship will blow up in your face, better to shift your lover's focus back to you by being mysterious yourself. Being proactive is infinitely better than being reactive. Let your charisma flow in such an abundance that not only your lover will notice, but so will everyone else around. Subtley let your partner know that you have the look, the fire, the focus, and the confidence to have anybody you want. But you choose to be with them. Although no plan is completely failsafe, this is a great way to remind them when they're facing temptation why they wanted to get with you in the first place. Therefore, the best way to get rid of your dog's flea problem is to spend less time worrying about them and to let them spend more time worrying about you!

Take A Bite Out Of Crime

The last thing that's required to continue your new romance heading down the road to success is to develop a keen sense of how to take a bite out of crime. Taking a bite out of crime refers to the way in which you handle any occasion where your new lover takes you for granted. When someone takes you for granted it is a form of disrespect. Your primary goal while involved in a liberating love affair is to keep a close watch on the level of respect maintained between the two of you. Respect is a prerequisite for love. If someone loses the respect they have for you, they can never develop a real love for you. If you have any intention of walking your dog all the way to the altar, defending the line of respect between the two of you is essential. Now is the time to start building for yourself a high level of esteem in the eyes of your new lover. Better to earn a reputation than to be given one.

For someone you care about to take you for granted is the same as committing a love crime against you. When you become aware of significant decisions being made by your partner that concerns the two of you without your consent, you should act swiftly and surely. You should act wildly! You should blow the whole thing out of proportion! You should go over the top with your response! Ordinarily, your lover will react to this the same as they would with any other emergency that could threaten the relationship, by immediately going on the defense. When they are thrown off balance and in a state of shock by your reaction you are automatically the one in control of the situation. And once in control of the situation, you can clearly communicate to your partner your sense of outrage over being callously taken for granted. For those who love to misunderstand, taking a bite out of crime does not in any way have anything to do with being physically violent. It does, however, have everything to do with verbally expressing your outrage over having been disrespected. Now these strategies should be used sparingly. Any flagrant misuse of these maneuvers will only result in weakening their potency in those instances when you really need them.

So obviously, the most effective way to walk your dog in public is to walk with confidence. Your ability to exude confidence is a major reason why your partner was attracted to you in the first place. If you can continue to walk in the same kind of confidence whenever you're together, then your odds of keeping them attracted increase significantly.

Chapter 8
Man's Best Friends

Friends. How many of us have them? Hopefully, the answer is all of us. That is, unless you're a recluse or a sociopath. What is a friend? Is a friend someone who always tell you what you want to hear? Is a friend someone who likes to do everything you like to do? Or, is a friend someone whom you have known for what seems like forever? The true definition of a friend is much broader than that. A friend is someone you know extremely well and are very fond of. In your eyes, they are an intimate associate. They are a very close acquaintance. A friend is an ally whom you can count on to remain on your side during whatever struggle you are experiencing. A friend is someone who is a supporter rather than a saboteur. For our purposes, the friends in question are platonic, not sexual. As much as some would like to have you believe, there is no such thing as "Fucking Friends". In fact, the two words are really mutually exclusive. There is no way for two people to keep being friends if they are also having sex. Eventually, one of the parties involved will feel the need to validate their frequent rolls in the hay by calling it a real, committed relationship. When this happen, the one who doesn't want a romantic relationship will head for the hills. This ends the friendship and the possibility of any romantic relationship that could have developed. This scenario doesn't always play itself out in this way, but most of the time it does. Sure, sometimes friends who indulge in casual sex decide to formerly make their relationship romantically official, but it's always a big gamble. Yes, the odds are stacked, and they're not in your favor. The best way for two people to stay friends and still have sex is to actually already be husband and wife. Enough said.

Marking Your Territory

It's always a good idea to do a little evaluating every now and then on whom you have chosen to call your friends. Are these people really the people you should listen to? What's their motives? What's their track record when it comes to romantic relationships? Can you trust them? Certain friends you'd trust with your money, your car, and even life. But you wouldn't dare trust them with your lover. Let's face it guys, certain friends you wouldn't let come near your little sister. Likewise ladies, there are certain friends of yours that you'd never let date your brothers because you know they'll dog'em out! It's true, there are people you may call friend whom you just can't trust around your girlfriend or boyfriend. To guard against any confusion, you have to mark your territory. Let your friends know how you feel about the special person in your life. Draw a boundary line around you and your romantic relationship that you expect your friends to respect. After the line has been made clear and your friends choose to cross it, then cross them out of your life! It may sound harsh, but there is no other way to protect the life of your romantic relationship. You have to let them know that they can't pee on your leg and trick you into thinking it's raining! It's not unheard of for many relationships to have ended as a direct result of outside interference coming from a so-called friend who wants the person you've got. If you are forced to cross some of these kinds of people out of your life, don't waste a lot of time shedding tears for them. People like these never have your best interest at heart in the first place. You never really suffer a loss when you lose counterfeit cronies.

To be aware of the company you keep is always a good thing. You can't help but come away with at least a part of everyone with whom you consistently associate. The more positive your friends are, the more positive you will be. Friends who habitually uplift, inspire, and motivate you add abundantly to your own energy reserves. Beware of the Fear of Petting Support Group.

The Fear of Petting Support Group

The Fear of Petting Support Group is not a group that meets every Tuesday at 2:00 p.m. at the psychiatrist's office. Instead, this is a very widespread group of men or women who meet every chance they get to badmouth the opposite sex. Perhaps you've seen them having meetings in bars, restaurants, coffee shops, and night clubs throughout the country. Maybe you've attended a few meetings yourself. Maybe you've even called a meeting and led the discussion yourself. But for the benefit of those who have never been to one, they can best be described as men-bashing and women-bashing sessions. If you listen in on one of these meetings you are bound to hear things like "All men are dogs, they can never be faithful!" or "All women are confused, they never know what they want!" If you are a card-carrying member of this support group, the last thing they ever want to see is someone actually find true happiness in a romantic relationship. To them, this is like a slap in the face. They consider it the ultimate rejection for one of their members to graduate from negativity to positivity. When you finally meet someone with whom you may actually have a healthy male and female relationship with, the nature of this new romance will dictate that you spend the time it takes to explore it's possibilities. The scene goes a little something like this: At first, you stop joining in when the bashing is in full effect. Then, you start wrecking the flow of all the negative stuff being espoused by trying to awkwardly say something positive about the opposite sex. Next, you start missing "scheduled" meetings because you start finding it increasingly hard to relate to the group's negativity since you are feeling so positive about your new romance. Soon, you start to feel kind of bad because now you've noticed they've stopped inviting you altogether. And lastly, you reach the point where you begin to realize that you don't miss those meetings at all!

Once you have successfully escaped from the Fear of Petting Support Group, you may find it possible to use your new positivity to get some of your old friends out too. Before you go on this particular kind of rescue mission, be sure to take a careful and realistic assessment of your fortitude. Remember, these are people who are just like you used to be. They have a fear of getting involved with the opposite sex because they think they'll only get burned again. Before you can be a positive influence on these kinds of people you must be sure you have built up enough of an immunity toward their negative dogma. To help them, you'll have to be strong. Until it finally sinks in to them that you are in a strong relationship, they'll periodically try to talk you out of it. Maybe they just miss you kickin' it with them as often as you used to. Maybe they don't mean to be so anti-relationship and they're just saying stupid stuff out of habit. Regardless, these friends of yours may continue to do this until they are successfully deprogrammed. Everyone has their own threshold by which they measure how long they should spend trying to salvage a friendship. If your friend tries to continuously sell you a busted bag of goods about how your good love is really bad love, you may be forced to cut them loose one last time.

The Think Tank
    When certain men get together and try to offer a friend advice on women, nothing good can come of it. A Think Tank is usually defined as a specialized group that comes together to research a problem intensely, swearing never to rest until it is solved. This definition, however, has absolutely nothing to do with the men described in the following story.

Doggietales: Curtis, age 30
    I can tell you right now that I ain't taking the blame for none of this. I remember when Jason first met that damn girl. It was all he ever talked about whenever we went out. I mean, we couldn't even meet at the sports bar and have a drink without talking about how great she was. How fine she was. How much in love with him she was. Well to tell you the truth, I wouldn't have minded it so bad if he would have just kept hanging with us. But, after a while, whenever we all went clubbing, he always made up some excuse not to come. One night we ran into him and his girl at a party. We were all surprised to see them there. I was more surprised than anybody, because I knew her. Jason's girlfriend was a girl I knew from back in high school. She was gorgeous then and she looked even better now. You've got to understand, back in high school I was the man! I was one of, if not "the", coolest guy in the whole school. I knew for a fact that Jason's girl, Nicollette, wanted to get with me back then. The only thing that saved her from being on my hit list was that I never got around to her. When Jason introduced her to us, me and her both played it off like we had never met before. After that day, we all met one Wednesday after work and had

135

ourselves a little conversation. The topic was whether or not a woman would cheat on the guy she was with after she was engaged. A couple of the fellas there were engaged, including Jason. It turns out that he had popped the question to Nicollette a few weeks ago. Of course, everybody had a different opinion about it. I told all the engaged guys that I could take any one of their ladies if I wanted to. They all generally told me I was crazy and laughed it off. But as things would turn out, one day Jason's girl stopped by my house looking for him. Jason had just left, but I invited her in anyway. I fixed her a drink and she admitted to remembering me from back in the day. We drank a little, talked about old times a little, and before I knew anything we were both handling our business in my bedroom! After it was over she tried to play that role like I took advantage of her while she was drunk. But we both knew that she wanted to get with me just like I wanted to get with her. Everything was cool for awhile, because we both kept what we did on the down low. One Friday night out with the guys though, I started running off at the mouth and I let it slip that I boned his girl. After that night, me and Jason stopped being friends. The next day, him and Nicollette stopped being engaged. I guess you can say I lost a friend. But really, I don't see it like that. If you ask me, I did him a favor by screwing Nicollette. It was the best way I could have shown him she was nothing but a little freak after all. Ain't that what friends are for?

Curtis' story is a good way to illustrate how important it is for you to choose carefully the people in your life you call friends. In this case, a Think Tank is a group of guys who get together and drink so much that the only thing that they can think of is something stupid. They are so "tanked" that they can't think straight. If you're a guy who thinks he can get good advice from a Think Tank, then you'd better think again!

The Brain Trust

Similar to men's Think Tank, women have a group of friends that sabotage their love lives too. We shall call theirs The Brain Trust. Ordinarily, a Brain Trust is defined as a group of experts that come together to act as advisors. This particular definition, like that of the Think Tank before it, has little to do with the women described in the following story.

Doggietales: Tanji, age35

I don't really know why we did it. I guess we just wanted our friend back. When Mari first met Drew, I guess we all thought he wasn't her type. I mean, he wasn't very outgoing at all. He was kind of conversative, so we all wrote him off as being nerdy. I guess it wouldn't have been so bad if we were there with Mari when she met him. Mari met Drew at a teacher's conference late last year. She said he was very nice and easy going. So when he asked her out and she said yes, the rest was history. We couldn't believe how Mari started acting. She started putting our plans on hold while she went out with Drew half the time. Even when she was out with us, she always made it her business to call Drew and tell him when she'd be home. We couldn't believe she was actually in love with this nerdy guy. Mari had really changed. It was like she was being brainwashed. She never used to make a move without us, but now she was acting totally independent. It was clear to us that something had to be done about this , so we started pointing out all the things about Drew that were less than perfect. Pretty soon, we had Mari believing that her Drew really was too good to be true. After enough times of us raining on her parade, we finally convinced Mari to stop seeing Drew. We finally got our girlfriend back. The only thing is, she still isn't the same. She never seems happy these days. It turns out that she really was happy with Drew. I guess he wasn't so bad after all. But now it's over. We helped kill it and now there's nothing that can be done about it.

With friends like Tanji, Mari has little use for enemies. Mari suffered tragically from listening to the advice of her Brain

Trust. She did, however, learn two things. First she learned that they had no brains. Then she found out that she sure couldn't trust'em!

The Best Friends

Much has been said about the worse friends, now let's touch briefly on the value of having the best of friends. As stated earlier, good friends are people who are always in your corner. The best friends are the ones who love you enough to not only tell you what you want to hear, but also what you need to know. Good friends don't engage in round table discussions at your expense. They care enough about you to know when to stop making the gossip rounds and to table all unflattering discussions. The funny thing is that the kind of friend you have been usually determines the kind of friends you get in return. What goes around really does come back around again. True friends will help support you in the things that you are doing right in your romantic relationship. When the day comes when you really need someone to have your back, your true friends will be there. They will remember how you looked out for them in the past, and will return the favor by looking out for you in the present. Never forget, the slack you cut your friends today could provide them with enough rope to pull your butt out of the fire tomorrow!

Chapter 9
Sit, Stay, or Rollover: When to let sleeping Dogs lie!

How do you know when you're in a deadend relationship? How do you know when your love life is all process and no progress? Is there one magic moment when you realize as you're climbing step by step up to new heights of love that you have your ladder leaned against the wrong wall? Or is it subtle things that give you little clues all along that you may need to let this sleeping dog lie.

It is said that hindsight is twenty-twenty vision, but you don't have to rely on hindsight if you keep your eyes wide open in the beginning. Many times, people would rather ignore relationship warning signs than heed than. In real life, as in good literature, foreshadowing is very important. The pleasures and problems of most relationships are often indicated beforehand. How some relationships ensue can often point the way to how they may conclude. The decision to stay or to go depends on you and what merit you place on the relationship.

Sometimes the decision to end a relationship is a direct result of what the person wanting out thinks a relationship is supposed to be. Are your expectations for long term romance realistic or unrealistic? Everybody wants a wedding, but who really wants a marriage? Wedding vows throughout history have been recited as a confirmation of the love and commitment to the betterment of a union that already exists. When the mere notion of exchanging vows with this person you're with comes as a shock or a major revelation to you, then you may have a big problem.

During the course of writing this book, many different reasons were given for ending relationships. The usual suspects that are rounded up include things like money, adultery, abuse, or lack of communication. More specifically though, the main cause of all relationship "deaths" is selfishness. Love of self in most respects is certainly a good thing. But too much love of self is the root of all break ups. When you find yourself showing an inordinate amount of concern for your own interests and having little or no concern for others, you are surely on the

141

wrong side of self-love. Selfishness is all-inclusive. It comes in His and Hers. When relationships end because of lack of compromise, somebody's selfishness is always the culprit.

The Storyteller Questions

    Relationships have a life of their own. It is a good idea from time to time to put them under the microscope. There is nothing wrong with giving your relationship an examination every now and then to see if you are getting your needs met, and if you are meeting the other person's. You can call it a romance checkup, if you will. If you consider yourself a mature person, and if you are serious about having a true love in your life, you have to examine your relationships. Understandably, the truth can sometimes be hard to face, but only if you fear it.

There are basically five questions you can ask yourself to determine whether or not you should stay in a relationship.

1. Are you happy now?
2. Would you advise your best friend to stay in a relationship like yours?
3. Have you been a pooper scooper for most of the relationship?
4. Would you want to see your son or your daughter in a relationship like yours?
5. If the person you're involved with never changed, would you be happy with them for the rest of your life?

However you answer these questions are crucial to your future love life. These questions are called Storytellers for a reason. It is because the answers you give to these questions will tell the story of your relationship. How you answer these questions will help you to discover the difference between pain and pleasure, lust and love, and action and achievement. The feeling of freedom and liberation that comes from gaining this knowledge cannot be overstated.

On the other hand, to resist this knowledge is to willingly surrender yourself into captivity. If you choose to put yourself and the well-being of your relationship totally in the hands of the other person, here's hoping you've chosen wisely. Many who have abdicated their will in relationships have found themselves being held hostage by an emotional terrorist. Emotional terrorists are men or women who'd love to manipulate you if you'd let them. These types love it when they can have you confusing accessibility with acceptability. If they can convince you how lucky you are to have them, then maybe you'll be too thankful to notice how much they're dogging you out in the relationship. If you're involved with someone like this and you're pretending that you're happy, it is the same as sticking your head in the sand. Remember, people who stick their heads in the sand also have their butts in the air. This, by the way, is the perfect position to be in to always get your ass kicked!

Knowing when to sit, stay, or rollover in a relationship a lot of times is a question of honesty. Being honest sometimes can be difficult. It takes guts to be honest when a lie would be much easier to tell. For many, lying is a way of life. People freely lie to each other as well as themselves. As a result, we live in a society where honesty is hardly ever heard. Honesty is a prized commodity that everybody wants to receive but they rarely want to give. The dishonesty that infests our personal relationships is also running rampant throughout our society. Today, so many scandals have resulted from the many lies told by publicly elected officials that they are pleading the fifth amendment just as much as organized crime figures. For those who don't know, the fifth amendment rights are pleaded by people in a court of law who make the statement, " I refuse to testify for fear that my testimony may incriminate me." Now, if it's true that elected officials represent us, and if their level of honesty is equal to that of mobsters, then that says a hell of a lot about who we are as people. Since we as a society go to great lengths to elect people who lie to us, is it any wonder we sometimes select lovers who will do the same? Never let nostalgia blind you from reviewing your relationship in it's entirety. Nostalgia is the enemy or true history. Sometimes history has only been kind to you because you have chosen to rewrite it. It is the main reason why people confuse quality of time in a relationship with quantity of time. Nostalgia turns you into a revisionist historian. It's always easy to think that the person you're with is great as long as you choose to remember the good times only. Judge the whole relationship, not just part of it. When you do this, you are being a historian with integrity. People who write history like to omit their own crimes and misdemeanors. They are always the protagonist, not the antagonist. It's always the fault of the girl that they're dating. Or, it's always the fault of the guy that they're

144

dating. Whenever they tell the story of how their relationships end, they're always the hero but never the villain. In truth, things are rarely that cut and dried. Although there is usually one person more guilty than the other, no one can claim to be entirely guilt free. Therefore, excessive finger pointing is a game that very few have a right to play.

Like it or not, the people we choose to become involved with come "as is". Sure, it is possible for people to change who they are given enough time, but you should never hold your breath waiting on it. Sometimes your own restlessness and immaturity can cause you to sabotage a good relationship. No one is perfect, so don't fall into the trap of holding the person you're involved with to a standard that you haven't reached yourself. To be as deeply involved in a relationship as you are, there had to be enough attraction and compatibility unifying you from the start. To kick somebody to the curb just because you're feeling bored right now is a sorry excuse to end a good relationship. You might only be bored with the relationship because "you're" boring right now. Change for change's sake is often stupidity, but deciding to stop being boring yourself is always a change for the better. Moods fluctuate, and your wants can be even more fickle. Choosing someone to spend the rest of your life with isn't a petty thing. It isn't as trivial as ordering at a restaurant. If you're thinking of getting rid of someone just because they're not perfect, then it's your seriousness about taking your relationship to the next level that's really in question. After all, if your lover really was perfect, then why would they want you? Seriously though, you can rest assured that if you have picked someone who complements who you are and gives you what you need, deciding whether to stay or go will be a very easy choice for you to make.

Chapter 10
Every Dog Has His Day

Are you a bad dog? Do you stay in the doghouse, willingly? Are you one of those people who let's their doggish tendencies run wild? Do you take pride in acting like an animal? Are you the type that takes their "animal" rights too seriously?

For those of you who aren't, this chapter may still prove educational. In this chapter, we'll attempt to find out who these type of people are, where they come from, and where they are going.

Who are they?

Bad dogs are people who can best be described as predators. They are out to please only themselves. They are the Kings and Queens of self-interest. To them, sex, money, and power are not only aphrodisiacs, they are absolutes. Love is much too abstract a concept for them to be concerned with at the moment. They live in the now, with total disregard for the past or future. And just like that PREDATOR in the movie, when they look at you they don't really see you at all. Just the heat rising off your ass! Their main mission is to get more butts than an ashtray. They are the married women who approach you in one aisle after they've sent their husband down the other. They are the guys who always tell you they love you just because they know that'll keep you around. It's not that these people don't know right from wrong, it's just that they don't care. They are the people who are ruled by their need for the constant challenge to achieve the next conquest, whoever or whatever that may be. They only want the things they can't have or shouldn't have. They are those who have a Peter Pan complex in the worst way. They have refused as yet to grow up emotionally and take responsibility for how what they do effects the other person. Somehow, they always enjoy the chase more than the catch.

The Making of a Bad Dog

Where do bad dogs come from? Do they create themselves or do others create them? Sure, some people are just rotten to the core from the start, but many times they are ruined as a result of their own bad experiences with relationships. It' an old story, but a true one, about how victims choose to become victimizers after their ordeal is over. Those who have been traumatized in the past have hearts that either stay too softened or grow too

148

hard. What are some of the things that harden a previously soft heart? What are some of the things that someone has done to you or either you have done to somebody else? Have you ever gave a guy the wrong number to call on purpose? Have you guys ever told a girl you'd call and never had any intentions of doing so? Then congratulations, this chapter's for you. As a matter of fact, the next bad dog you meet might also be for you. This could be your payback for the bad dog's you've helped to create. Some of us really are responsible for creating enemies for the next guy or girl.

Although the examples named may seem minor in comparison to major relationship scandals like cheating with your lover's best friend, but they are given just to illustrate how seemingly little things can do terrible damage. When enough damage is done, the person who was on the receiving end may start to change their views on the value of the opposite sex. They start to think of potential lovers more like chewing gum than candy. Candy is sweet and consistently tasty. It dissolves within you, and as you digest it, it becomes a part of you. Chewing gum, on the other hand, is sweet and tasty for only a short period of time. After it loses it's flavor, it is designed not to be digested but to be discarded. Therefore likewise, to a bad dog, people are not to be kept and cherished, but to be used and thrown away. These bad dogs refer to the people they're sexually intimate with as friends so as not to call it what it really is. That way they can maintain "squatter's rights" with one prospect while all along keeping their options open.

The Reversal of a Bad Dog

It is always true that every dog has his day. There is a time when what goes around, indeed comes back around. No matter what path is chosen in life, every road has to end somewhere. Historically, the bad dog lifestyle leads to various deadend roads. Sometimes they meet someone who really loves them but they are too desensitized to recognize it or appreciate it. Or sometimes, they simple tire of dogging people out and just marry anybody just to settle down. But most of the time they fall prey

149

to the Canine Equation. The Canine Equation is a formula that was inspired by a series of movies that hit theaters one particular year. The movies were Booty Call, Love Jones, and Sprung. Booty Call, for the sake of those who might have missed it, is a movie about people out looking only for sex. Love Jones was a movie about people who weren't looking for love, but fell hopelessly into it anyway. And lastly, Sprung was a movie about people who were in love and didn't have any idea how to handle it, but were much too entangled to escape it. **The Canine Equation** is BC+ LJ= S. Bad dogs who are in the habit of making booty calls eventually may come down with a love jones and end up sprung! Such has been the fate of many a bad dog.

All dogs go to heaven?

It's a fact that all dogs can go to heaven, but only if they change their ways. After time starts to take it's toll, they become too old to run with the big dogs like they used to. Before this happens though, many who have been living like it's no tomorrow start to really contemplate the future. People can change. It just usually takes a crisis situation to make some old dogs want to learn new tricks. It is not uncommon for a person to change their life once they realize they are routinely experiencing more pain than pleasure. If someone wants to change bad enough, they find the tools necessary to help them achieve this. Yes, every dog has his day. Could this day be a good day for you to change?

151

Chapter 11
Every Dog Has His Day Part 2, or They'll Never Stop making Lassie Movies

Have you ever noticed how many movies about dogs there are? Every time you turn around, some movie studio has released a new film about a lovable canine. From Lassie, to Benji, to Air bud, everybody loves a good dog. The lesson to you here is that even if you have not found the love you want in your life yet, keep your head up. As long as you commit to keep looking, you may find that love is just around the corner. Perhaps you feel that you have been hurt one time too many and fear that you might never love again. If your heart was true and you were in it to win it, then you should have no regrets because you will most certainly love again. Remember, all good dog movies have sequels.

Someone with a lot of wisdom once said that there are no new experiences, they are just new to you. We are, in effect, going thru the same old things for the first time. As has been said before, people come into our lives for a reason, a season, or a lifetime. As long as there is life, there is another chance to love. If you are alone, there is no law that says you have to feel lonely. If you have been hurt, use the time alone to love yourself and learn from the past. Don't succumb to the temptation to lower your standards and start settling for less. Don't start petting mongrels when you know your heart isn't in it. If you dabble in this practice and you finally meet someone you're compatible with while you're doing this, then you won't be fully available for them. In order to get out of your meaningless relationship,you will have to dog the other person out. This will make you guilty of being as much a villain as the person who dogged you out previously. To become what you hate the most in other people is a crushing blow to the person you have worked so hard to become. A clear conscience is worth the trouble it takes to maintain. Don't dog anybody out. That way, if you can't sleep at night it won't be because of guilt. Take time to lick your wounds and heal. If you can't run with the big dogs again just yet, it's alright sometimes to stay on the porch. Your day in the sun is coming soon.

If you've been thru a bad breakup, there are three steps you can take to get over it.

The first thing necessary to move on with your life is to allow yourself to recall exactly what happened. Don't ignore it, don't suppress it or bury it like hazardous chemicals or toxic waste. Toxic waste doesn't always stay buried. Oftentimes it resurfaces and poisons our rivers and water supply. Likewise, don't allow bad memories to resurface and poison any new relationship you might enter into. Remember them, then deal with them.

Secondly, you have to relinquish your hold on the bad memories. Let them go. Let the person who hurt you go, too. Don't bear them ill will or carry a grudge. Holding grudges is too much work to do. It is better to forgive. When we don't forgive, it's not the other person that ends up going thru hell, it's us. Don't be a mudslinger. You can only be losing ground if you're always slinging mud. Don't waste your time.

Thirdly, you have to come up with a new way of looking at your past experience. You must look hard enough to see the value in having survived the breakup. The new meaning that you glean from it must be educational. Surely there are things that you have learned from the experience that you can use to grow to a new level of understanding. If you can learn from the past, maybe there'll be no need to repeat it. Sometimes it can't be avoided. We all grow our tallest during times of trial and tribulation. Farmers have always known that a surefire way to get a seed to grow was to throw manure on it. Isn't it about time that we too admit that nothing makes us grow quite like going thru crap? Recognize that the past is in the past, it does not have to be your future. What happens to us is almost never as important as what happens in us.

Love

What is love? Many people who are asked have been unable to define it. And if one cannot define it, how can one recognize it? There are thousands of words in the English language. Some are polysyllabic while others are monosyllabic. There was a time when the hardest three words to say were " I love you", but that's now no longer the case. People say it all the time now. They throw it around today very casually. "I love you." Everbody interprets it differently. As long as it's undefined it can remain vague enough for everybody to attach their own meaning.

What is love, really? Love is more than simple physical attraction. Human love that leads to marriage seems to be a peculiar mixture of sexuality and selflessness. The physical half of the love equation is easiest to grasp. It's not hard to understand wanting to be with one particular person more than anyone else. There's nothing mysterious about a desire to want to be in that person's corner and to help them to be all they can be in every area of life. It is that facet of love that allows you to comfortably give that other person the total freedom to be themselves and still have affection for them anyway that is so unfathomable.

The Bible defines love not so much by what it is, but by what it does. First Corinthians chapter thirteen describes love as being patient and kind. It is said to be never envious or jealous. It is never full of pride or holds grudges. Love is always on the side of right and against what is wrong. Love is boundlessly strong, everlasting, and completely unfailing.

Another way that the Bible describes love is by who it is. According to the scriptures, God is love. Therefore, a possible definition of true love is the experience of being so genuinely attracted to another person that you are willing to allow God to love them thru you. This is the kind of love we all yearn to give and receive. This is your goal. It is attainable if you never give up. There's still lots of happy marriages in the world today. It's just that you never hear about them because good news rarely makes the news.

True love starts with loving who you are. You can't give of what you don't have. Unless you are dedicated to loving yourself first, you will find it difficult to accept it from someone else. Only when you are comfortable with sharing the love you feel for yourself with others can you expect to get it in return. So stop being afraid. Get out there and get what you want. Every great thing in life really worth having comes with at least a small bit of fear linked to it. That's the obstacle we all must overcome to get what we really want. Love is a prize that you have to be willing to run the race to win. Crossing the finish line through faith, despite the fear we may feel, is what we all must do to celebrate in life's winning circle. Having the guts to fly into the face of fear is what earns you the right to enjoy life's greatest prize... LOVE.

Decide today that this is your day to take action because now you have options. Now you are prepared and knowledgeable. Preparation has given you confidence that has increased your peace of mind. The Doggiestyle strategies have armed you with an arsenal of arrows you can use to help you shoot for the love you've always wanted. Good hunting!

The Doggiestyle Dictionary

1. Attack Dogs - People you meet who are so desperate for love that they pounce on you. They are prone to be somewhat obsessive.
2. Brain Trust - A group of women friends whose sole purpose for coming together is to screw up the love life of whichever one of them happens to be in a good relationship.
3. Canine Equation - Also known as the K-9 Equation. The formula is BC+ LJ = S. Bad dogs who are in the habit of making Booty Calls eventually come down with a Love Jones and end up Sprung.
4. Challenge Stage - That point in every relationship where one person pulls away in order to decide whether or not they want to stay.
5. Diner Sex - A cheap, falsified love affair that gives the appearance of a real relationship, but really is just a front for casual sex.
6. Dog - A word used to describe that part in everybody that is only concerned with self-appeasement.
7. Doggiestyle - the name of the book you're holding in your hands. Also, it is a colloquial term used to describe a whole new style of approaching dating.
8. Doggy Bag Effect - leftover morsels that other people give to the person you're dating that only serve to remind them of you. These morsels are things either said or done that leave an impression on the person you're dating once they hear it.
9. Drive-Thru Sex - the preferred type of sexual rendezvous for those who like to hit and run just for fun. It is a close relative to the Booty Call.
10. Dumb Dogs - People you meet who aren't bright, or at least for a brief moment in time, don't act too bright.
11. Fleas - Anybody who tries to attach themselves to the person you're dating for the purposes of taking them away from you.
12. Hot Dogs - People who are only out for sex.
13. Hunting Dogs - Folks who are out to romance as many men or women as they possibly can. As soon as they capture the

heart of one person, the need for a constant challenge drives them onward to the next.

14. Junkyard Dogs - People who show disrespect or disregard for their things and the things of others.
15. Law of Mutt Magnetism - the law that states that if a person enters into new relationships before taking the necessary steps to counteract the harmful effects of love affairs from the past, they are destined to attract people into their lives who will hurt them the same way.
16. Multiplicity Effect - The phenomena that occurs when one person can be in two places at once.
17. Mutt Magnets - Men and women who attract people into their lives that mean them absolutely no good.
18. Network Principle - A strategy that some use to reel in dates by throwing out as many flirtatious lines as possible.
19. Penitentiary Love - That warped, suffocating, and confining type of relationship that many feel pressure to escape from.
20. Pooper Scoopers - Individuals who are habitually cleaning up, covering up, or hiding all evidence that they are being dogged out in their relationship.
21. Rabid Dogs - Those who are still infected with pain and resentment from their past relationships.
22. Rabies Shot - The recovery steps that everyone must take before they are ready to start a new relationship after an old one has ended.
23. Scooby Snacks - Rewards that you give the person you're with after they have been exceptionally good to you.
24. Show Dogs - Folks who are in the dating world who either like to see a show or put on one.
25. Storyteller Questions - A set of pointed questions that you ask yourself that will tell you exactly what kind of relationship you really have.
26. Stupid Pet Tricks - Humiliating or shameful things that people who aren't Top Dog in their relationships do out of desperation to keep their partner from leaving them.
27. Think Tank - A group of guys who come together solely for the purpose of thinking up new ways to stop each other from entering into any serious relationships with women.

28. Third Date Abracadabra - A magic trick that occurs the moment you notice that the object of your desire has started to transform into a real person. It is the general moment when fantasy gives way to reality.
29. Tied Dogs - People who would love to date you even though they are already involved, engaged, or married.
30. Top Dogs - People who are on top in their relationships. They are people who always try to respect the sanctity of their relationships. They stay on top in the relationship because they know that no one is supposed to be on the bottom.
31. Under Dogs - People who allow themselves to be treated like second-class citizens in their relationships because of their own lack of self-respect.

About The Author

Steven Eric Scruggs is known in many circles as a Complete Artist. He is a talented Writer, Cartoonist, and Songwriter based in Memphis, Tennessee. His intentions for writing Doggiestyle are to offer to the hungry dating world a relationship, how-to book that they can really sink their teeth into! His exhaustive knowledge on the subject of relationships come from over ten years of intentional and unintentional research. As a bachelor fighting to survive in the dog eat dog world of dating, Steven felt that it was time for someone to finally write a book that tells the truth about what really works and what doesn't. Before Doggiestyle, there existed no concise definitions of a lot of things we do in pursuit of finding real love. Now, with the wisdom, the humor, and the artistic clarity that only he can so uniquely bring to the table, that's all changed!

Doggiestyle is here!